The Hunter Writing System

Sentence Sense

Skills Practice Book— with Paragraph and Essay Exercises

Red Level

Form A

Anthony Devereux Hunter, Sr.

Hunter & Joyce Publishing Company
Delhi, New York

THE STANDARD SERIES:

THE HUNTER WRITING SYSTEM: SENTENCE SENSE, RED LEVEL
[The "red" level is the INTRODUCTORY LEVEL.]

The Hunter Writing System: Sentence Sense, Green Level
(September 1995) [The "green" level is the INTERMEDIATE LEVEL.]

This *Skills Practice Book* contains the practice material for its companion text, which is a separate work and has an accompanying teacher's guide. It also contains paragraph and essay practice material.

ORDERING INFORMATION:

CALL: **800-745-3377 (800-7 4-KEEPS) or 607-746-3196**

WRITE: **Hunter & Joyce Publishing Company**
R.R. 2, Box 54
Delhi, NY 13753

ANTHONY DEVEREUX HUNTER, SR. has taught English for twenty-nine years and Latin for one year in junior and senior high schools and in colleges in the United States. In addition, he has taught English as a second language overseas for three years. He has conducted many workshops in the area of grammar and writing.

COVER: The layout for the cover is the work of Scott Jensen.

Printed in the United States of America
ISBN: 0-9625839-6-0

To the Teacher

This is **not** a stand-alone work.

The primary purpose of this *Skills Practice Book (Red Level)* is to provide the exercise material for its companion work *The Hunter Writing System: SENTENCE SENSE (Red Level)*, which is the "text." Note that ALL THE TEACHING AND EXPLANATORY MATERIAL—relative to sentence writing skills—ARE IN THE TEXT and that the page references of this *Skills Practice Book* (after its Contents pages) are to the text.

A second purpose of this text is to supply enough paragraph and essay exercise material to comply with the objectives of writing programs.

All students should have their own copy of this *Skills Practice Book*. This will enable them to devote their undivided attention to achieving the goals of the exercises as they carry them out.

All students should also have a copy of the companion text to study from as well. That book's graphic material and examples have been designed to give **visual** reinforcement to its instructional content.

A.H.

Contents

Chapter 1

Background for Understanding Verbs

Practice A: IDENTIFYING TYPES OF SENTENCES

[From text, page 2]

DIRECTIONS: These sentences are either questions, statements (sentences that you can turn into a question), or commands. Label the type that each is by circling the **Q** for QUESTIONS, **S** for STATEMENTS, or **C** for COMMANDS. Note that all verbs have been darkened for you. Imitate the example.

Example: **Has** the noon whistle **blown** ? ((Q) · S · C)

1. **Walk** quickly. (Q · S · C)
2. **Has** it **started** to rain? (Q · S · C)
3. The skunk **had slipped** into our garage. (Q · S · C)
4. **Will** everyone **get** a turn? (Q · S · C)
5. The door **has been closed** tightly. (Q · S · C)
6. **Leave** that up to me. (Q · S · C)
7. **Watch** your step. (Q · S · C)
8. The plans **were changed** at the last minute. (Q · S · C)
9. Some bees **have been living** inside this tree. (Q · S · C)
10. **Can** everyone **hear** easily? (Q · S · C)

Practice B: DISTINGUISHING BETWEEN SENTENCES AND DEPENDENT CLAUSES

[From text, page 3]

DIRECTIONS: Each line contains either a sentence or a dependent clause. Each also has a darkened word. If you can shift the darkened word to the front and cause a question, circle the answer **S** (FOR SENTENCE). If you cannot do this shifting, circle the answer **DC** (for DEPENDENT CLAUSE). Be sure to keep the darker word **covered** in its inside-the-sentence position as you do your testing. Imitate the example.

Example: When the sun **had** set. (S · (DC)) [**had** when the sun ~~**had**~~ set]

1. Because he **had** left his milk money at home. (S · DC)
2. The answers **must** be supplied by you. (S · DC)
3. Everyone **has** done the memory work. (S · DC)
4. Since the train **will** arrive on time. (S · DC)
5. If you **have** never gone that far South. (S · DC)
6. When the nights **are** cloudless. (S · DC)
7. The horse **would** whinny before breakfast time. (S · DC)
8. Wildflowers **can** brighten the appearance of a field. (S · DC)
9. After all the tests **were** corrected. (S · DC)
10. Battery-run clocks **are** unaffected by lightning. (S · DC)

Practice C: IDENTIFYING MAIN VERBS IN A VERB PHRASE

[From text, page 7]

DIRECTIONS: For each of the sentences in this passage, place the letters **MV** over every MAIN VERB. Note that all the verbs have been darkened for you. Imitate the example.

MV
Example: The sun **will have set** by then.

When a farmer **is haying** his field, he **must proceed** in an orderly way. First, he **must cut** the hay. Then he **will spread** it so it **can dry** faster. Finally, he **will wrap** it in bales for storage. When he **is working** in the field, he **will drive** his tractor in circles from the outside of a field to the center until the whole field **has been given** the treatment in question. You **can be** sure that he **will be praying** that no rain **will interfere** with his work.

Practice D: IDENTIFYING HELPING VERBS IN A VERB PHRASE

[From text, page 7]

DIRECTIONS: For each of the sentences in Practice C, place the letters **HV** over every HELPING VERB. Imitate the example.

HV HV MV
Example: The sun **will have set** by then.

Practice E: IDENTIFYING ONE-WORD MAIN VERBS

[From text, page 7]

DIRECTIONS: For each of the sentences in this passage, write **MV** over the MAIN VERB. The verbs have been darkened for you. Imitate the example.

MV MV
Example: We **won** today after Carlos **hit** a double.

The coach of our Little League team **started** the season poorly. He **believed** that players **belong** where he **puts** them. He **refused** to hear our complaints. He even **benched** the pitcher, our best player, after he **finished** his three innings. Our team **lost** the first two games because of this. Then somehow he **got** some sense. Now we **have** a chance to take first place.

Practice F: IDENTIFYING MAIN VERBS AND HELPING VERBS

[From text, page 7]

DIRECTIONS: For each of these sentences, place the letters **MV** over every MAIN VERB and **HV** over every HELPING VERB. Note that all the verbs have been darkened for you. Imitate the example.

MV HV HV MV

Example: The bat that **broke** last night **has been discarded**.

1. The downpour **blinded** drivers and **pelted** them with hail.
2. As dusk **sets** in, birds **will sing** their evening songs.
3. When appliances **work** properly, homeowners **can become** overconfident.
4. Businesses now **use** computers whose power **could** not **have been imagined** four years ago. [*Could have been imagined* is one verb.]
5. When the roads **become** rivers, potholes **can** only **become** larger. [*Can become* is one verb.]
6. Those who **study** while they **watch** TV **will do** less effective work.
7. Everyone **should know** the easier knots that Boy Scouts **learn**.
8. Friendship **should mean** more than possessions that just **accumulate**.
9. Most ball-point pens **must be thrown** away while fountain pens just **need** refilling with ink.
10. Someone who **visits** Europe in spring **will be surprised** at how long daylight **lasts** there.

Practice G: SUPPLYING COMPONENT SPELLINGS FOR SIMPLER VERBS

[From text, page 12]

DIRECTIONS: Fill in the blanks for these verbs. Note that you form the spellings for their components in the same way that you form the spellings for the verb ***want***. The first item has been answered for you as a model.

	BASIC	S/ES	ING	PAST TENSE	AFTER-HAD
1.	**list**	lists	listing	listed	listed
2.	**call**	______	______	______	______
3.	**pull**	______	______	______	______
4.	**laugh**	______	______	______	______
5.	**talk**	______	______	______	______
6.	**like**	______	______	______	______
7.	**lack**	______	______	______	______
8.	**surprise**	______	______	______	______
9.	**blink**	______	______	______	______
10.	**stray**	______	______	______	______
11.	**pour**	______	______	______	______
12.	**drain**	______	______	______	______
13.	**imagine**	______	______	______	______
14.	**follow**	______	______	______	______
15.	**pretend**	______	______	______	______

* * * * *

PARAGRAPH AND ESSAY SUPPLEMENT

INTRODUCTION ... AUTOBIOGRAPHY

FOR USERS OF THIS MINI-TEXT

- **Content in boxes is information of general importance.**
- **All shaded material is of extra importance.**

Paragraph

A PARAGRAPH is one or more sentences whose chief purpose—as a main building block of longer pieces of writing—is to state and (usually) develop a topic related to the whole work. Paragraphs are always indented—that is, their first word is inset a detectable amount from the left-hand margin (the left edge) of the writing. The statement of its topic idea is commonly found in its first sentence and has the name TOPIC SENTENCE.

Topic Sentence

The sentence at the start of a paragraph that announces and controls what you will say.

Standard Procedure for All Chapters of This Mini-Text

1. **Prepare an OUTLINE (as the first step in all writing efforts):**
   a. **State the point to be discussed—in informal wording;**
   b. **List the details or proof—in informal wording;**
   c. **Arrange the order of the points (to help the reader);**
2. **WRITE YOUR PARAGRAPH/ESSAY BASED ON YOUR PLAN (leave extra spacing between lines for corrections):**
   a. **Turn the "point to be discussed" into a TOPIC SENTENCE;**
   b. **Add old/new details to complete each paragraph.**
3. **Read (aloud) what you have written to catch any errors.**
4. **Rewrite your work, ALWAYS CORRECTING AND IMPROVING IT.**

Help for the Student

- **In outline examples, bold and capitalized lettering highlights every "point to be discussed."**
- **In paragraph examples, bold and capitalized lettering highlights every topic sentence.**
- **In essay examples, bold and capitalized lettering highlights topic sentences AND titles, introductions, and conclusions.**

GOAL IN THIS MINI-CHAPTER

To prepare and write the story of your life—one paragraph at a time.

Practice H: PLANNING A PARAGRAPH ON WHAT YOU ARE MOST PROUD OF

DIRECTIONS: Decide what in your life you are MOST PROUD OF (an accomplishment, a performance, an act of kindness or heroism, or a reward you received). (Alternatively, you can speak about what you are most proud of with respect to someone close to you.) First SAY WHAT HAPPENED (the "point to be discussed"). Then LIST THE DETAILS—the circumstances, timing, place, and so forth—that can help the reader better understand the event. Imitate the example outline supplied below.

Example Outline

I AM PROUD OF MY SKILL WITH A BB GUN
A single-pump gun
Had to adjust it for built-in errors
Would aim at spools on a ledge
Would get them with the first shot

Practice J: WRITING A PARAGRAPH ON WHAT YOU ARE MOST PROUD OF

DIRECTIONS: Write a paragraph based on the outline that you prepared in Practice H. Imitate the example paragraph supplied below.

Example Paragraph

I AM QUITE PROUD OF THE SKILL I ACQUIRED WITH A SINGLE-PUMP BB GUN. *Because the sights for this gun were inaccurate, I had to make adjustments in the height and width of my aim. As time went on, I was able to shoot down a row of threadless spools—that were quite thin in the middle—just about at will. I would be standing about twenty-five feet away.*

Practice K: PLANNING A PARAGRAPH ON SOMETHING MEMORABLE OR SPECIAL

DIRECTIONS: Now pick out something in your life that is especially MEMORABLE or SPECIAL. It could be something especially important or unusual; it could be something joyful or sad; it could be something in the present or in the past. (Alternatively, you can speak about what was/is especially memorable or special with respect to someone close to you.) First SAY WHAT HAPPENED (the "point to be discussed"). Then LIST THE DETAILS—the circumstances, timing, place, and so forth—that can help the reader better understand the event. Imitate the example outline supplied below.

Example Outline

CAUGHT AT FAR END OF LAKE IN CANOE BY SELF ON WINDY DAY

Heavy canoe
Was paddling from the stern
Sped to end of lake
Couldn't turn the canoe into the wind
Felt trapped
Need to paddle from the front explained by rescuer

Practice L: WRITING A PARAGRAPH ON SOMETHING MEMORABLE OR SPECIAL

DIRECTIONS: Write a paragraph based on the outline that you prepared in Practice K. Imitate the example paragraph supplied below.

Example Paragraph

I WILL NEVER FORGET THE DAY I ENDED UP IN A CANOE AT THE WRONG END OF A LAKE. *I had gone paddling by myself and was good at steering a canoe from the back seat. This day the wind was strong, and the canoe was one of the heavier kinds. The ride to the end of the lake—the far end—was smooth and fast because the wind was behind my back. When I got to the end, though, the wind was so strong that I could not make the boat face the wind so I could paddle back up the lake. When help finally arrived, after a tear or two as I recall, I learned that you have to paddle from the front of a canoe in a heavy wind.*

Practice M: PLANNING A PARAGRAPH ON A MEANINGFUL EXPERIENCE

DIRECTIONS: Now pick out something in your life that is especially MEANINGFUL to you. It could be what others praise you for or remember you for. It could be what you want to be remembered for. (Alternatively, it could be something especially meaningful in the life of someone close to you.) First SAY WHAT HAPPENED (the "point to be discussed"). Then LIST THE DETAILS—the circumstances, timing, place, and so forth—that can help the reader better understand the event. Imitate the example outline supplied below.

Example Outline

I OUTSCORED MY SISTERS & BROTHER ON A STATEWIDE GEOGRAPHY EXAM

Was a rivalry, each trying to beat out the others
Was a different exam every year
My 96 the best of all grades
Mine the easiest exam (according to them—and in fact)
Still the best of all the scores

Practice N: WRITING A PARAGRAPH ON A MEANINGFUL EXPERIENCE

DIRECTIONS: Write a paragraph based on the outline that you prepared in Practice M. Imitate the example paragraph supplied below.

Example Paragraph

MY OLDER SISTERS, BROTHER, AND I HAD A RIVALRY OVER OUR GRADES ON THE STATE EXAMS AT THE END OF A YEAR. *When my turn came to take the geography exam, they had no reason to believe I would beat them. I guess I did not think I would either. However, I did. To this day, they complain that my exam was easier than theirs. They are right, but I am still the one who got a 96.*

Practice P: PLANNING A PARAGRAPH ON A HOBBY OR INTEREST

DIRECTIONS: Now pick out a hobby or interest of yours that occupies some or a lot of your time or attention. (Alternatively, you can speak about a hobby or interest of someone close to you.) First SAY THAT YOU HAVE THIS PARTICULAR HOBBY OR INTEREST (the "point to be discussed"). Then LIST THE DETAILS that can help the reader better understand how much the hobby or interest means to you. Imitate the example outline supplied below.

Example Outline

MY STAMP COLLECTING HOBBY GAVE ME AN EDGE IN GEOGRAPHY
- *Not sure when started*
- *Was bought stamps by my father*
- *Spent many hours arranging my stamps and admiring them*
- *Marveled at their colorfulness, differences, and shapes*
- *Learned something of history and geography in the process*

Practice Q: WRITING A PARAGRAPH ON A HOBBY OR INTEREST

DIRECTIONS: Write a paragraph based on the outline that you prepared in Practice P. Imitate the example paragraph supplied below.

Example Paragraph

ONE EDGE I HAD OVER MY SISTERS AND BROTHER IN THE AREA OF GEOGRAPHY WAS MY DEEP INTEREST IN STAMP COLLECTING. *I became absorbed in them because of their beauty, variety, shapes, and differences. I would buy packages of stamps and spend hours sorting them according to country and time period. I would have others save them for me, and my father would buy some at the post office for me from time to time. Curiosity over the location and history of the countries in question made me use maps and ask more questions than my sisters and brother ever did, I suspect.*

Chapter 2

Nouns and Their Replacers

Practice A: USING THE *THE* TEST—TO FIND NOUNS

[From text, page 16]

DIRECTIONS: Use the THE Test for Finding Nouns to find the nouns in this paragraph. Place the letter **N** over each NOUN that you find. Imitate the example.

N N N
Example: The computers of our day have magical qualities.

The office of the future will have a computer at its hub [*center*]. Beside the computer, it will have a device that prints. Workers will sit at stations where they will use typewriter-like keyboards and monitors. Some machines will require the insertion of waferlike discs before they perform certain functions. The repairman of the computer will replace the repairman of the typewriter.

Practice B: IDENTIFYING PROPER NOUNS

[From text, page 20]

DIRECTIONS: Label all the PROPER NOUNS in this passage by placing the letter N over each. Where a proper noun is two (or more) words long, you can place a brace (⏜) over the group so that you need only one N. Imitate the example.

N N N N

Example: My friend Bill Heathwood lives in Colorado Springs, Colorado.

Recently a youth from Baronne, France, named Philippe Dumond visited us in Delhi, New York. He and a friend Paul Duvoir had two weeks left to reach their places of work in Napa Valley, California, and Redmond, Oregon, respectively. They decided to hitchhike despite the fact that we had urged them to use safer means of travel.

Philippe has since written about his part of the trip. They reached Ohio right away but experienced bad luck after that, mostly because they were together. From Chicago on, they traveled separately. After Philippe reached Des Moines, Iowa, he was picked up by a person named Jim, who supposedly was heading for Los Angeles, California. While Philippe was asleep one night at a stop-over in the Rocky Mountains, Jim robbed and abandoned him.

When Philippe awoke and could not find his wallet, he was desperate. Fortunately, the town of Glenwood Springs, Colorado, was nearby. With the help of the police there, he was wired enough money to finish the trip, which he did—by bus.

Practice C: IDENTIFYING MORE NOUNS

[From text, page 20]

DIRECTIONS: Now place an N over ALL THE OTHER NOUNS in the paragraphs in Practice B.

Practice D: IDENTIFYING PERSONAL PRONOUNS IN THEIR BASIC/"SUBJECT" SPELLING

[From text, page 24]

DIRECTIONS: For this passage, place a **triangle** around EACH PERSONAL PRONOUN. Imitate the example.

Example: My brother and I had bought a present together, but he hid it so well that we could not find it.

You and I have been blessed. We live in a country where we have freedom. Other peoples live under dictators. They can be arrested for what they believe, for gathering in groups, for going to church, and for many other reasons. We must appreciate what we have.

He—or she—who values freedom will struggle to preserve it.

Practice E: IDENTIFYING PERSONAL PRONOUNS IN THEIR SPELLINGS AS "OBJECTS"

[From text, page 25]

DIRECTIONS: For this passage, place a **triangle** around ALL PERSONAL PRONOUNS—both basic ones and those in their "object" spelling.

When our friends and we go camping, lots of belongings come with us. They have a huge box, which we share. They place it on the roof of their car. In it, everyone places the sleeping gear, food, and cooking utensils. We pack them tightly.

They do not bring the dog or the cat. They leave him to guard their house and her to catch mice. They leave them in the care of their neighbors who feed them.

It takes us hours to reach the mountains. We love it there, though, and return often. Wouldn't you if you could try it?

Practice F: IDENTIFYING PERSONAL PRONOUNS IN THEIR SPELLINGS THAT INDICATE OWNERSHIP

[From text, page 26]

DIRECTIONS: For this passage, place a **triangle** around ALL PERSONAL PRONOUNS—those that are basic, those in their "object" spelling, and those that indicate ownership.

In an organized family, people and things have set places. At dinner time, Dad gets his food at one end of the table. Mom gets hers opposite Dad. The children get theirs where they usually sit. I get mine where I sit by a window; you would get yours beside me if you were my guest. The dog gets his by the washer; the cat gets hers upstairs. (The mice get theirs if there are crumbs anywhere.)

If our family were a guest of yours, we would get ours wherever you placed us.

Practice G: IDENTIFYING PERSONAL PRONOUNS IN THEIR SPELLINGS THAT "SELF-NAME"

[From text, page 27]

DIRECTIONS: For this passage, place a **triangle** around ALL PERSONAL PRONOUNS—those that are basic, those in their "object" spelling, those that indicate ownership, and those that indicate "self."

We place ourselves at risk if we disregard rules and common sense. My father puts himself at risk if he arrives at work late. My mother puts herself at risk if she does not concentrate on her [adjective] driving. My sister and I put ourselves at risk if we do not do our [adjective] homework right away. Our friends put themselves at risk when they jog on the wrong side of the road. You put yourself at risk when you ride your [adjective] bike on the wrong side of the road. I put myself at risk when I disregard a fever. A bird puts itself at risk when it flies headlong into a window.

Practice H: IDENTIFYING ALL PERSONAL PRONOUNS

[From text, page 27]

DIRECTIONS: Return to Practice B. Place a **triangle** around ALL THE PERSONAL PRONOUNS in those paragraphs. Try to exclude the words that serve as adjectives. Imitate the example.

Example: He placed his coat near mine. [*His* is an adjective; you can say *his coat*.]

Practice J: IDENTIFYING PRONOUNS, ESPECIALLY INDEFINITE PRONOUNS IN THEIR -ONE/-THING/-BODY FORMS

[From text, page 28]

DIRECTIONS: Place a **triangle** around ALL THE PRONOUNS in this passage.

Summer seems as if it has everything when it is arriving. It seems to have had nothing when it is over. When someone says something to somebody about summer, everyone wants everybody to have everything all over again.

If anyone wants anybody to appreciate anything about summer, he should not mention it in midwinter. In midwinter, nothing seems less appropriate: nobody cares; everyone wants none of it.

Practice K: IDENTIFYING PRONOUNS, ESPECIALLY INDEFINITE PRONOUNS IN THE "OPPOSITES" AND "MISCELLANEOUS" GROUPS

[From text, page 29]

DIRECTIONS: Place a **triangle** around ALL THE PRONOUNS in this passage.

Many of us like to exercise; few dislike it altogether. Each gets exercise differently. One jogs; another does aerobic dancing; others swim; some play tennis; all walk. Much is gained by exercise; little—except pounds—is lost.

Most of us get plenty of exercise. The ones who get the most are the ones who keep the healthiest. Each of us should try several of the types of exercise. Both of the most common types, walking and running, are healthful. Either will benefit you; neither should harm you.

Practice L: IDENTIFYING PRONOUNS, ESPECIALLY INDEFINITE PRONOUNS

[From text, page 29]

DIRECTIONS: Place a **triangle** around ALL THE PRONOUNS in this passage.

When something goes wrong with people's bicycles, they must ask whether someone has ridden them besides themselves or whether nothing but lack of maintenance is at fault. Anything that goes untended will deteriorate. Everything requires maintenance from time to time.

Either of two choices is available. One can care for a bike, or one can neglect it. Some do the first of these; others do the second. Few of the people I know neglect their bikes entirely. Many, like myself, give them extra care; few give no care of any sort.

Much of what people do will be the result of how important they think maintenance is. Little is done if motivation is lacking. Anybody who knows anything will agree to that. Nobody could deny it.

I find none of the above statements to be untrue. Someone once said, "Leave nothing to chance." Another has said, "Where there's a will, there's a way." Keep this in mind when you have your own bike.

Practice M: IDENTIFYING PRONOUNS, ESPECIALLY DEMONSTRATIVE PRONOUNS

[From text, page 30]

DIRECTIONS: Place a **triangle** around ALL THE DEMONSTRATIVE PRONOUNS in this passage.

Andrew made up a schedule for the week. It occurred to him to do this last night. He made time for his chores. These he squeezed between times for playing. He left himself choices too. Those were for the times when the weather might be bad or a friend might be away.

This is something new for him to try. He wondered whether he would stick to the schedule. That remains to be seen. That depends on where he puts it and whether it means very much to him.

Practice N: IDENTIFYING MORE NOUNS AND PRONOUNS

[From text, page 30]

DIRECTIONS: Place the letter **N** over all nouns and a **triangle** around ALL REMAINING PRONOUNS in the passage in Practice M.

PARAGRAPH AND ESSAY SUPPLEMENT

FRIENDLY LETTER

GOALS IN THIS MINI-CHAPTER

To use correct format for writing a friendly letter, to prepare an outline as a plan for a letter, and to practice letter writing.

PRACTICE P: PLANNING A FRIENDLY LETTER

DIRECTIONS: Write an outline for a friendly letter to anyone you might wish—an old friend; a favorite aunt, uncle, or cousin; a former teacher; or anyone. For things to discuss, plan paragraphs about your friends, what is happening in your life, your accomplishments, your plans, or any other subject that you would like. Select at least three of these. For each such topic, write a statement that can serve as "point to be discussed." Then list the details that indicate what you will say. BEFORE these, write out the word "introduction" and indicate what you might say to start your letter. AFTER the paragraphs with your topics, write out the word "conclusion" and indicate what you might say to bring your letter to a close. Imitate the example outline supplied below.

Example Outline

INTRODUCTION: ***THIS IS JUST TO SAY HELLO***

EVENTS WHEN JOGGING:
Huge truck behind me
Afraid I would give up
Fragrance of the ferns by the road
Uphill victory
Help for studying

EVENTS AT BREAKFAST:
Forgot Andy's birthday
Remembered all of a sudden
Couldn't find my favorite cereal

EVENTS LATER IN THE DAY:
Unusual bird sighting—or just an oriole?
Irises by window
Humidity with a cool breeze

CONCLUSION: ***KEEP IN TOUCH***

Practice Q: WRITING A FRIENDLY LETTER

DIRECTIONS: Write out a letter based on the outline you prepared in Practice P. Be sure to turn each "point to be discussed" into a topic sentence—that is, a sentence that both announces and controls all that follows in that paragraph. Imitate the example letter—including the format—supplied below.

Example Letter

15 Clover Lane
Bridgeport, MA 11587
June 29, 1994

Dear Jim,

I AM JUST WRITING TO LET YOU KNOW I AM THINKING OF YOU AND TO SHARE WITH YOU A FEW THINGS THAT HAPPENED TO ME JUST THIS MORNING.

I WENT JOGGING BEFORE BREAKFAST AS USUAL. *When I heard a heavy truck behind me, I went as far to the edge of the road as possible and finally stopped to look. It was an oil truck that was so wide it hogged two thirds of the road! I found running harder than I expected—it was humid—but I kept going. As I passed through a wooded area, the fragrance of the damp ferns was most pleasant. And on the way down, I got an insight that will help my studying.*

AT BREAKFAST, I WAS CLUELESS. *It was Andy's birthday, but he wasn't letting on. Finally, I remembered on my own—but it was a close one. All I could think of was that we had no more of my favorite cereal left!*

NOT MUCH ELSE IS HAPPENING HERE EXCEPT THAT I DID SEE A BIRD THAT I THINK IS A NEW ONE FOR ME. *It was as big as a robin but had yellow striping on its breast; and when it flew, its tail feathers spread wide and looked yellow-orangish. It may have been a female Baltimore oriole, but I am inclined to think it was some bird I have not seen before.*

ANYWAY, LET ME HEAR FROM YOU SOON.

Your brother,

Hal

Practice R: PLANNING AND WRITING ANOTHER FRIENDLY LETTER

DIRECTIONS: Follow the directions for both Practice P and Q above, but write a different letter. You may write to the same person or to someone else.

Chapter 3

Introduction to Agreement of Verbs with Their Subjects

Practice A: IDENTIFYING SINGULAR AND PLURAL NOUNS AND PRONOUNS

[From text, page 36]

Directions: Over each of the darker words in these sentences, write an **S** if it is SINGULAR IN NUMBER or a **P** if it is PLURAL.

The **way** of **living** of a **person** affects his **surroundings**. **Someone** who is reluctant to throw **things** out will find **piles** of **junk** everywhere that **he** or **she** turns. On the other hand, **those** who quickly sort and dispose of unnecessary **belongings** find that **they** can keep their **rooms** appearing orderly. Unhappy, however, is any **person** who has thrown out what **he** or **she** needs in order to study for coming **tests** and final **exam**.

Practice B: IDENTIFYING THE PERSON OF NOUNS AND PRONOUNS

[From text, page 40]

DIRECTIONS: For each of these sentences, write **1**, **2**, or **3** over each darker word to indicate the "PERSON" for that word.

1. Light **reading** is helpful if **you** want to read faster or widen your vocabulary.
2. When **someone** races downhill, **he/she** risks an injury.
3. When **we** arrived at the campsite, **I** helped with the unpacking.
4. Though **houses** may also be expensive, the **cost** of borrowing from the bank can be even more expensive.
5. **I** don't remember why **you** were not there.
6. When **they** reached the river, **Zach** was the first one in.
7. **We** decided that each **person** should get a chance at bat.
8. **One** must decide whether **he/she** is in school to have fun or to make something of him-/herself.
9. The **teacher** has not told us when **we** will be tested.
10. When **Louise** found her book, **she** discovered that **it** was overdue.

Practice C: MORE IDENTIFYING OF SINGULAR AND PLURAL NOUNS

[From text, page 40]

DIRECTIONS: For each of the sentences in Practice B, write **S** or **P** over **each darkened word** to indicate whether its "NUMBER" is SINGULAR (**S**) or PLURAL (**P**).

Practice D: MAKING VERBS AGREE WITH THEIR SUBJECTS

[From text, page 43]

DIRECTIONS: In each blank space, write out the correct spelling for the verb (supplied in parentheses).

1. Pete (prefer/prefers) ___________ tennis to baseball.
2. A person of good character (enjoy/enjoys) _____________ genuine happiness.
3. Professional games sometimes (last/lasts) ______________ overlong.
4. Some R-rated movies (belittle/belittles) ________________ the types of people portrayed.
5. Gardens (need/needs) ______________ plenty of water.
6. Winter sometimes (arrive/arrives) _______________ abruptly.
7. Many girls (dislike/dislikes) ________________ hunting and fishing.
8. Cars (seem/seems) ___________ to be more and more costly.
9. A student soon (learn/learns) _____________ to listen well.
10. A good driver (anticipate/anticipates) __________________ problems.

Practice E: REWRITING A PARAGRAPH USING CORRECT AGREEMENT

[From text, page 43]

DIRECTIONS: Fill the blank spaces in this paragraph. Choose either ***he*** or ***she*** as subject for each sentence, and spell each VERB so that it **AGREES** WITH its SUBJECT. The subjects are in darker letters; the verbs are in parentheses. Also choose either ***his*** or ***her*** throughout to be consistent with the ***he*** or ***she*** that you choose.

A sensible **student** (guard) _________ the alertness of his/her mind. **He/she** (calculate) ______________ how he/she can get the amount of sleep **he/she** (need) _________. **He/she** (refuse) ____________ to drink any alcoholic beverage. **He/she** (eat) _________ three meals a day and (seek) _________ out those foods that are needed for health, such as vegetables, fruits, and protein-rich foods. **He/she** (avoid) __________ drugs as being the poison they are. **He/she** frequently (choose) ____________ a sport or exercise that forces fresh air into his/her lungs to freshen his/her mind. **He/she** (know) ________ that missing a class can be like having a chapter missing from a book.

Practice F: Using the Verb *Be* Correctly in the Present Tense

[From text, page 44]

Directions: Fill each blank with the correct **PRESENT TENSE COMPONENT SPELLING** for the verb *BE*. Choose only ***AM, IS,*** or ***ARE***. Note the example.

Example: I __am__ telling you where you __are__.

I ______ sure that you ______ the person I should tell this to. A person who ______ tired can have a change of personality. He ______ often grouchy. He finds fault with others. He ______ hard to live with. He ______ often ashamed of how he behaves. I ______ sure that you ______ someone who has experienced this too. I ______ always easier to live with when I have had enough sleep. I ______ sure that you ______ too.

The members of my family ______ in agreement with me. They ______ eager for me to get enough sleep. They ______ always more sure of my disposition when I have had enough rest.

Practice G: Using the Verb *Be* Correctly in the Past Tense

[From text, page 45]

Directions: Fill each blank with correct **PAST TENSE COMPONENT SPELLING** for the verb *BE*. Choose only ***WAS*** or ***WERE***. Note the example.

Example: I __was__ here when they __were__ here yesterday.

It ______ 4:15 when the storm arrived. I ______ in the car with my father. He ______ heading for home. Other drivers ______ on the road too. The sky ______ so dark that it ______ like dusk.

Rain fell. It ______ so thick and so heavy that my father instinctively slowed down. Then it ______ hail and rain that fell. Fewer cars ______ on the road now. Headlights ______ on. People ______ turning off the road. It ______ a frightening scene. We ______ late getting home, but we ______ glad to have arrived safely.

PARAGRAPH AND ESSAY SUPPLEMENT

MEMORANDUM

GOAL IN THIS MINI-CHAPTER

To practice using a standardized form of communication, a memorandum.

MEMORANDUM

A MEMORANDUM is a short note to someone to express a concern, a complaint, or a compliment. Because you use a standardized form (see below), you avoid the need for an introduction and conclusion.

PRACTICE H: PLANNING A MEMORANDUM

DIRECTIONS: Prepare an outline for a one-paragraph memorandum. Direct your memorandum to a coach, a teacher, a principal, a mayor, a president, a supervisor or other person for whom you have an important message. Tell the person about, possibly, IMPROVEMENTS needed in pricing of some item(s), graffiti, energy wastage, curfews, noise, study (hall) conditions, cafeteria concerns, and so forth—**or** pay the person a COMPLIMENT or EXPRESS YOUR THANKS. State your main point (the "point to be discussed") first. Then add the details and/or proof that supports it. Imitate the outline model supplied below.

Example Outline

ARCHER HILL ROAD HAS DANGEROUS SWELLINGS THAT NEED CORRECTION
Between Thompson's and Larner's
Cause people in the back seat to hit the ceiling
Have rises of at least a foot
Can cause harm to cars and trucks
Are unavoidable if drivers stay on own side of road
Unavoidable going uphill or downhill
Need immediate attention

Practice J: WRITING A MEMORANDUM

DIRECTIONS: Write a memorandum based on your outline in Practice H. Imitate the example memorandum below **and** its format.

Example Memorandum

TO: *Supervisor of Highways* **DATE:** *July 1, 1994*

FROM: *Clarence Stodges*

SUBJECT: *Hazards on Archer Hill Road*

THIS WINTER HAS CAUSED A SERIOUS DETERIORATION OF ARCHER HILL ROAD BETWEEN THOMPSON'S AND LARNER'S. *There are now four rises or bumps at least a foot high and wide enough that they are unavoidable by drivers who stay to their side of the road. These bumps are so severe that a back-seat passenger hits the ceiling—whether the driver is heading uphill or downhill. They could break the springs or shocks on a car or truck. These hazardous rises need your immediate attention.*

Practice K: PLANNING AND WRITING A SECOND MEMORANDUM

DIRECTIONS: Write an OUTLINE and a ONE-PARAGRAPH MEMORANDUM that are like the examples above. Imitate the layout too. Direct your memorandum to a camp counselor, parent, guardian, or other person in charge. Tell the person about problems that need his/her attention in any of these areas (or similar ones): chores, allowances, rules, timing, fairness, supervision, and so forth. In your outline and essay, make your point and support it with details and/or proof—**or** pay the person a compliment or express your thanks.

Chapter 4

More Information about Verbs

Practice A: Supplying Component Spellings for Irregular Verbs with Five Spellings

[From text, page 49]

Directions: Fill in the blanks for these verbs. Note that you must **know** the spellings for the past tense and after-had components. For the PAST TENSE SPELLING, **use the word in** a sentence of your **own WITH *YESTERDAY***. For the AFTER-HAD SPELLING, **say the word AFTER *HAD***. Imitate the verb *sing*, which has been done for you.

	Basic	S/ES	ING	Past Tense	After-had
1.	**sing**	**sings**	**singing**	**sang**	**sung**
2.	arise				
3.	awake				
4.	bear				
5.	begin				
6.	bite				
7.	blow				
8.	break				
9.	choose				
10.	do				
11.	draw				
12.	drink				
13.	drive				
14.	eat				
15.	fall				
16.	fly				
17.	forbid				
18.	forget				
19.	freeze				
20.	get				
21.	give				
22.	go				
23.	grow				
24.	hide				
25.	know				

Practice B: More Supplying of Component Spellings for Irregular Verbs with Five Spellings

(From text, page 49)

Directions: Fill in the blanks for these verbs. Follow the same directions that were given for Practice A.

Basic	S/es	Ing	Past Tense	After-had
1. lie (recline)	__________	__________	__________	__________
2. mistake	__________	__________	__________	__________
3. ride	__________	__________	__________	__________
4. ring	__________	__________	__________	__________
5. rise	__________	__________	__________	__________
6. see	__________	__________	__________	__________
7. sew	__________	__________	__________	__________
8. shake	__________	__________	__________	__________
9. shrink	__________	__________	__________	__________
10. sing	__________	__________	__________	__________
11. sink	__________	__________	__________	__________
12. speak	__________	__________	__________	__________
13. spring	__________	__________	__________	__________
14. steal	__________	__________	__________	__________
15. stink	__________	__________	__________	__________
16. swear	__________	__________	__________	__________
17. swim	__________	__________	__________	__________
18. take	__________	__________	__________	__________
19. tear	__________	__________	__________	__________
20. throw	__________	__________	__________	__________
21. wake	__________	__________	__________	__________
22. wear	__________	__________	__________	__________
23. weave	__________	__________	__________	__________
24. write	__________	__________	__________	__________

Practice C: SUPPLYING COMPONENT SPELLINGS FOR IRREGULAR VERBS WITH FOUR SPELLINGS

[From text, page 49]

DIRECTIONS: Fill in the blanks for these verbs. Note that you must **know** the spellings for the past tense and after-had components. For the PAST TENSE SPELLING, use the word in a **sentence of your own** WITH *YESTERDAY*. For the AFTER-HAD SPELLING, **say the word** AFTER *HAD*. Imitate the first one, which has been done correctly for you.

	BASIC	S/ES	ING	PAST TENSE	AFTER-HAD
1.	**tell**	**tells**	**telling**	**told**	**told**
2.	bend	______	______	______	______
3.	bind	______	______	______	______
4.	bleed	______	______	______	______
5.	bring	______	______	______	______
6.	build	______	______	______	______
7.	buy	______	______	______	______
8.	catch	______	______	______	______
9.	cling	______	______	______	______
10.	creep	______	______	______	______
11.	deal	______	______	______	______
12.	dig	______	______	______	______
13.	dwell	______	______	______	______
14.	feed	______	______	______	______
15.	feel	______	______	______	______
16.	fight	______	______	______	______
17.	find	______	______	______	______
18.	flee	______	______	______	______
19.	fling	______	______	______	______
20.	grind	______	______	______	______
21.	hang	______	______	______	______
22.	have	______	______	______	______
23.	hear	______	______	______	______
24.	hold	______	______	______	______
25.	keep	______	______	______	______

Practice D: SUPPLYING COMPONENT SPELLINGS FOR IRREGULAR VERBS WITH FOUR SPELLINGS

[From text, page 50]

DIRECTIONS: Fill in the blanks for these verbs. Imitate the first one, which has been done correctly for you.

	BASIC	S/ES	ING	PAST TENSE	AFTER-HAD
1.	**bring**	**brings**	**bringing**	**brought**	**brought**
2.	kneel	________	________	________	________
3.	lay	________	________	________	________
4.	lead	________	________	________	________
5.	leap	________	________	________	________
6.	leave	________	________	________	________
7.	lend	________	________	________	________
8.	light	________	________	________	________
9.	lose	________	________	________	________
10.	make	________	________	________	________
11.	mean	________	________	________	________
12.	meet	________	________	________	________
13.	pay	________	________	________	________
14.	say	________	________	________	________
15.	seek	________	________	________	________
16.	sell	________	________	________	________
17.	send	________	________	________	________
18.	shine (glow)	________	________	________	________
19.	shoot	________	________	________	________
20.	sit	________	________	________	________
21.	sleep	________	________	________	________
22.	slide	________	________	________	________
23.	sling	________	________	________	________
24.	spend	________	________	________	________

Practice E: STILL MORE SUPPLYING OF COMPONENT SPELLINGS FOR IRREGULAR VERBS WITH FOUR SPELLINGS

[From text, page 50]

DIRECTIONS: Fill in the blanks for these verbs. Imitate the verb *say*, which has been done for you.

	BASIC	S/ES	ING	PAST TENSE	AFTER-HAD
1.	**say**	**says**	**saying**	**said**	**said**
2.	spin	______	______	______	______
3.	spit	______	______	______	______
4.	stand	______	______	______	______
5.	stick	______	______	______	______
6.	sting	______	______	______	______
7.	strike	______	______	______	______
8.	sweep	______	______	______	______
9.	swing	______	______	______	______
10.	teach	______	______	______	______
11.	tell	______	______	______	______
12.	think	______	______	______	______
13.	understand	______	______	______	______
14.	weep	______	______	______	______
15.	win	______	______	______	______
16.	wind (curve)	______	______	______	______
17.	wring	______	______	______	______

Practice F: SUPPLYING COMPONENT SPELLINGS FOR IRREGULAR VERBS WITH THREE SPELLINGS

[From text, page 51]

DIRECTIONS: Fill in the blanks for these verbs. Imitate the verb *cost*, which has been done for you.

	BASIC	S/ES	ING	PAST TENSE	AFTER-HAD
1.	**cost**	**costs**	**costing**	**cost**	**cost**
2.	bet	________	________	________	________
3.	bid (offer)	________	________	________	________
4.	broadcast	________	________	________	________
5.	burst	________	________	________	________
6.	cast	________	________	________	________
7.	cost	________	________	________	________
8.	cut	________	________	________	________
9.	forecast	________	________	________	________
10.	hit	________	________	________	________
11.	hurt	________	________	________	________
12.	let	________	________	________	________
13.	put	________	________	________	________
14.	quit	________	________	________	________
15.	read	________	________	________	________
16.	rid	________	________	________	________
17.	set	________	________	________	________
18.	shed	________	________	________	________
19.	shut	________	________	________	________
20.	slit	________	________	________	________
21.	spread	________	________	________	________

Practice G: Identifying Components for the Verb *Be*

[From text, page 52]

Directions: Double underline all the COMPONENTS OF THE VERB ***BE*** that you find in this passage. Note that all verbs have been written in darker lettering. Use the last line of the chart on page 51 of your text as a guide.

Example: Everyone **has been told** what the rules **are.**

Carlos **is** my brother. We **are** good friends. I **am** at a loss when he **is** not around. Once when we **were fishing,** a huge fish **was nibbling** on his line. But he **was being distracted** by a rabbit. The fish that **had been nibbling** got away. He **has been** unhappy over that ever since. He **was** not **being** a good fisherman that day. We **were** both disappointed. Whenever we **are** near that stream, he **is** the first to say that he **was** foolish that fateful day in June.

Practice H: Test of Knowledge of After-Had Spellings for Irregular Verbs

[From text, page 52]

Directions: Read each sentence for sense. Then fill each blank space with the **CORRECTLY SPELLED COMPONENT FOR THE VERB** (in parentheses) before it. Note how the example has been done.

Example: It is not (know) ___known___ who will be (give) ___given___ awards.

1. If he had (speak) __________ while on the ladder, he might have (fall) __________.
2. Even the candy that had been (hide) __________ behind the picture was quickly (find) __________ by the older children.
3. We would have (drive) __________ if we had (know) __________ that it was this far.
4. If the concert had (cost) __________ less, more would have (come) __________.
5. They have (drink) __________ everything that was (bring) __________.
6. No one who has (fly) __________ in a jet can have (forget) __________ the experience.
7. If she had been (choose) __________ for the part, it would have (be) __________ ideal.
8. No picture I have (draw) __________ has ever (win) __________.
9. If he had (see) __________ how much his pants had (shrink) __________, he would have (go) __________ back and (wear) __________ something else.
10. Last Sunday, we (lose) __________ the map that we had (buy) __________.

Practice J: WRITING SENTENCES THAT EXPRESS A COMMAND

[From text, page 54]

DIRECTIONS: Write THREE short **sentences of your own THAT EXPRESS A COMMAND**. Do **not** add the word *you* in front of the verb. Imitate the example. Note that the verb in the example has been darkened for you.

Example: **Aim** for the best possible grades.

____

____

____

Practice K: MORE IDENTIFYING OF TYPES OF SENTENCES

[From text, page 54]

DIRECTIONS: These sentences are either questions, statements (sentences that you can turn into a question), or commands. Label the type that each is by circling the **Q** for QUESTIONS, **S** for STATEMENTS, or **C** for COMMANDS. Note that all verbs have been darkened for you. Imitate the example.

Example: **Can** a student **turn** a wrong answer into a gain ((Q) · S · C)

1. The brook **has become** a river (Q · S · C)
2. **Stop** at once if the red light **comes** on (Q · S · C)
3. Will someone **answer** the phone (Q · S · C)
4. Do not **interrupt** important conversations (Q · S · C)
5. A blue heron **is** a bird that **eats** fish (Q · S · C)
6. **Do** leaves **turn** before it **starts** to rain (Q · S · C)
7. Abundant rain **helps** trees grow bigger (Q · S · C)
8. **Allow** extra time for longer writing assignments (Q · S · C)
9. **Start** longer assignments right away (Q · S · C)
10. A homeowner **can ruin** a machine instead of fixing it if he **has** no instructions (Q · S · C)

Practice L: WRITING SENTENCES USING THE BASIC SPELLING TO FORM THE PRESENT TENSE

[From text, page 56]

DIRECTIONS: Write THREE **sentences of your own** that use a verb's **BASIC** COMPONENT to form its **PRESENT TENSE**. Note the example (the verb is in darker and capitalized lettering).

Example: Trees **BEND** in the wind.

____

____

____

Practice M: WRITING SENTENCES USING THE S/ES SPELLING TO FORM THE PRESENT TENSE

[From text, page 56]

DIRECTIONS: Write three sentences of your own that use a verb's **S/ES** component to form its **PRESENT TENSE**. Note the example (the verb is in darker and capitalized lettering).

Example: Careful work **REQUIRES** time.

____

____

____

Practice N: WRITING SENTENCES USING THE PAST TENSE

[From text, page 57]

DIRECTIONS: Write three sentences of your own that use a verb's **PAST TENSE** component to form its **PAST TENSE**. Note the example (the verb is in darker and capitalized lettering).

Example: The rain **FORMED** puddles.

____

____

____

Practice P: WRITING SENTENCES USING THE FUTURE TENSE

[From text, page 57]

DIRECTIONS: Write three sentences of your own that use the helper ***WILL*** and a verb's **BASIC** component to form its **FUTURE TENSE**. Note the example (the verb is in darker and capitalized lettering).

Example: The sun **WILL REAPPEAR** soon.

____

____

____

* * * * *

PARAGRAPH AND ESSAY SUPPLEMENT

TENSES

GOAL IN THIS MINI-CHAPTER

To practice writing paragraphs in the present, past, and future tenses.

Practice Q: PLANNING A PARAGRAPH IN THE PRESENT TENSE

DIRECTIONS: Prepare an outline for a paragraph in which you will use ONLY the present tense. For the "point under discussion," state something that you do—or someone else does—THAT IS UNIQUE OR OF SPECIAL INTEREST. Then, for the benefit of a friend/brother/parent/classmate, list the details of what you do (or this other person does) when carrying out this activity—an activity such as camping, driving, biking, cooking, racing, strolling, or whatever. Imitate the example outline supplied below.

Example Outline

SHOPPING FOR THE BEST PRICE AT THE GROCERY STORE:

Pricing the store brand
Pricing the no-name brand
Cost-per-ounce comparisons
Mismarked items
Last week's items
Taking advantage of the "percentages"

Practice R: WRITING A PARAGRAPH IN THE PRESENT TENSE

DIRECTIONS: Write a paragraph based on the outline you prepared in Practice Q. Imitate the example paragraph supplied below. Use ONLY THE PRESENT TENSE.

Example Paragraph

WHEN I SHOP, I SEARCH CAREFULLY FOR THE BEST PRICE I CAN FIND. *I am not reluctant to buy the store's brand or a no-name brand. I compare the cost per ounce for both smaller and larger size cans, bags, or boxes. I even search for mismarked items or items with last week's sale price still on them. I look for these behind the items that are outermost on the shelf. I figure that a 10% savings is better in my pocket than in someone else's. Over the months, I save a great deal of money.*

PRACTICE S: PLANNING A PARAGRAPH IN THE PAST TENSE

DIRECTIONS: Prepare an outline for a paragraph in which you will use ONLY the past tense. For the "point under discussion," mention an INTERESTING EXPERIENCE that you or someone else had. Then, for the benefit of a friend/brother/parent/classmate, list the details of what happened to you (or to this other person). Then list the details of the incident, such as all the circumstances surrounding it and any lesson to be learned. Imitate the example outline supplied below.

Example Outline

LOST IN MOUNTAINS

Set out near where we were staying
Couldn't determine where we were
No stream
Climbed to where we could see below us
Recognized the road
Got back very late

Practice T: WRITING A PARAGRAPH IN THE PAST TENSE

DIRECTIONS: Write a paragraph based on the outline you prepared in Practice S. Imitate the example paragraph supplied below. Use ONLY THE PAST TENSE.

Example Paragraph

WHEN I WAS MUCH YOUNGER, I GOT LOST ON A MOUNTAIN. *I was with my younger brother in the Adirondack Mountains in New York. After we started to climb the mountain that was near to where we were staying, we lost our sense of direction. At first, we looked for a stream, but there was none. Finally, we climbed to the top and looked down to see if anything was familiar. Fortunately, we recognized the part of the road that was visible. We arrived back safely but many hours later.*

Practice U: PLANNING A PARAGRAPH IN THE FUTURE TENSE

DIRECTIONS: Prepare an outline for a paragraph in which you will use ONLY the future tense. For the "point under discussion," mention to a friend (or anyone of your choosing) something that either you are planning or would like to be planning—whether it is something you will be a collector or owner of; or a vacation or project you are planning; or an achievement or goal (for now or later in life) that you have set your heart on. Then list the details of what it is you are planning or would like to be planning. Alternatively, write about what someone else is planning. Imitate the example outline supplied below.

Example Outline

FATHER TO START A BUSINESS
- *To remodel the garage*
- *To buy needed equipment: computer, copier, etc.*
- *To do phoning*
- *To advertise*
- *To tell friends*

Practice V: WRITING A PARAGRAPH IN THE FUTURE TENSE

DIRECTIONS: Write a paragraph based on the outline you prepared in Practice U. Imitate the example paragraph supplied below. Use ONLY THE FUTURE TENSE.

Example Paragraph

MY FATHER WILL START HIS OWN BUSINESS SOON. *First, he will convert his garage into an office. Then he will buy a computer, a printer, a fax machine, a copier, and all the software he will need. He will also spend a lot of time on the phone. Finally, he will advertise a lot and will tell all his friends his plans. He will be a success if people will buy his services.*

Chapter 5

Helping Verbs

Practice A: LABELING STARTERS FROM THE *DO* SET

[From text, page 62]

DIRECTIONS: **Double underline** all the STARTERS from the ***DO*** SET. Note the example.

Example: When Mom **does** cook often, we **do** eat well often.

1. When we do try our best, our teacher does appreciate it.
2. Though Al did try, he did not succeed.
3. Since Carol does sing well, the others do rely on her too much.
4. When we do learn the answers, we do not always profit from them.

Practice B: LABELING STARTERS FROM THE *HAVE* SET

[From text, page 63]

DIRECTIONS: **Double underline** all the STARTERS from the ***HAVE*** SET. Note the example.

Example: If you **have** promised, you **have** given your word.

1. Though the sun has shone for hours, snow has now been predicted.
2. Since we have come this far, we have half finished.
3. Though the answer that Joanne had given satisfied the teacher, few in the class had really heard it.
4. When rugs have not been vacuumed, sand has sometimes ruined them.

Practice C: LABELING STARTERS FROM THE *DO* AND *HAVE* SETS

[From text, page 63]

DIRECTIONS: **Double underline** all the STARTERS from the ***DOES*** and ***HAVE*** SETS.

1. Jack has done so well that he has made the honor roll.
2. Whoever asked that had failed to listen carefully enough.
3. It does help a class when students have tried their best.
4. Though we had listened and had taken careful notes, we did not reread the notes afterward.
5. Though teachers do appreciate neat handwriting, they do not say this often enough.
6. Since Jill has made other plans, we have asked Marge to come.

Practice D: LABELING STARTERS FROM THE *BE* SET

[From text, page 64]

DIRECTIONS: **Double underline** all the STARTERS from the ***BE*** SET.

1. I am sure that no one was at fault.
2. The reason for the delay is that there were too many in line.
3. Are scientists as certain of their theories as we assume?
4. Was Jo's anger pretended, or is she truly upset?

Practice E: LABELING STARTERS FROM THE *DO, HAVE,* AND *BE* SETS

[From text, page 64]

DIRECTIONS: **Double underline** all the STARTERS from the ***DO, HAVE,*** and ***BE*** SETS.

1. Is Ellen the person who has borrowed my sunglasses?
2. If Jim is still here, I am going to tell him myself.
3. Though we had returned there, we were unable to find the gloves.
4. There are many reasons why everyone does not get the grades that he has wished.
5. Since Barb had the better recipe, she was the one who was chosen to bake the cake.
6. Whoever has written this editorial does choose effective wording.
7. When we have tried our best, we have already achieved something.
8. Since no one is sure of everything, all are able to be wrong.

Practice F: Labeling Starters from the *Will* Set

[From text, page 66]

Directions: Double underline all the starters from the ***Will*** Set.

1. A lawn mower that can cut normal grass quickly might stall and sputter in overgrown grass.
2. We shall see whether the five-day weather forecast will hold up.
3. How easily can someone find out what the exact time might be?
4. We must decide soon whether the advantages of owning a computer would sufficiently offset its cost.
5. Could the reason for Len's wrist alarm ringing be that he forgot to turn it off?
6. It may not be long before the effect of robots on the job market can be judged.
7. Since the air will be humid, we should be grateful that it will be cooler.
8. When we can smell salt in the air, we must be approaching salt water.

Practice G: Labeling Starters from the *Do, Have, Be,* and *Will* Sets

[From text, page 66]

Directions: Double underline all the starters from the ***Do, Have, Be,*** and ***Will*** Sets.

1. If a person can find lifetime work that he enjoys, he will be happy at what he is doing.
2. Since few can say that they have always been helpful at home, they should consider how much their parents have helped them.
3. If Will could spell better, he would like writing more.
4. If I may offer a word of advice, bicyclists must never let their eyes become too absorbed in the scenery.
5. Whenever youngsters do behave as they have been told, they are rewarded at least by a sense of satisfaction with the self-control that they have used.
6. What has been completed is not as much as was needed.
7. Those who had stayed were told, but those who did not stay are still uninformed.
8. Unless I am mistaken, Carol was not even told when she should return the book that she had borrowed.
9. I shall see whether this might earn me an A.
10. We may as well see whether we could be doing something that would be more useful than just sitting around.
11. Though a tractor has great power, it can get so mired in mud that it is without any power at all.
12. A pencil that has lost its eraser may well have lost the part that was most valuable.

Practice H: LABELING STARTERS IN CONTRACTIONS WITH *NOT*

[From text, page 68]

DIRECTIONS: Double underline ALL STARTERS. Imitate the example.

[will not]
Example: A dog that ^ won't bark at strangers wouldn't be much of a watchdog.

1. Wouldn't a house that is too airtight be more dangerous than one that isn't?
2. The freezer that we had wanted to buy wasn't small enough that we could squeeze it through the door.
3. If it doesn't rain soon, many wells will run dry.
4. Each day that has gone by may be a clearer sign that our entry hasn't won the contest.
5. Since she hadn't left herself extra time, Martha couldn't complete her report before the deadline.
6. When Steve studies, he won't turn his stereo off.

Practice J: REWRITING CONTRACTIONS OF STARTERS WITH SUBJECTS

[From text, page 69]

DIRECTIONS: Change each contraction in this passage to the TWO WORDS that it stands for. Imitate the example.

[it has] [who is] [we will]
Example: If **it's** ^ come down to **who's** ^ the best at spelling, **we'll** ^ have a contest.

If it's all right with you, I'd like to say something. For years, I've watched my own children grow. They've done chores when asked. They've even washed a dish or two. However, they're never around after a meal with guests. They'll vanish to their rooms or elsewhere. They've decided that all that mess is Mom's and Dad's responsibility. They'll let them be the adults.

There's room for change. They've got to realize when they've reached college age that volunteering when the going's roughest is the surest sign of maturity.

Practice K: LABELING STARTERS THAT COME FROM CONTRACTIONS WITH SUBJECTS

[From text, page 69]

DIRECTIONS: **Double underline** EACH OF THE STARTERS IN PRACTICE J. Note that some starters will be part of contractions and others will not. Imitate the example.

Examples: If **it's** ^ [it has] come down to **who's** ^ [who is] the best at spelling, **we'll** ^ [we will] have a contest.

You **may** be surprised at who **can** spell the best.

Practice L: MORE LABELING OF STARTERS THAT COME FROM CONTRACTIONS WITH SUBJECTS

[From text, page 69]

DIRECTIONS: **Change each contraction** in this passage to the TWO WORDS that it stands for. At the same time, **double underline** EACH OF THE STARTERS. Also **double underline** ALL OTHER STARTERS. Imitate the examples above.

Around our house the rule's always been that no cat's to be allowed. Mom's word was final. After all, an animal's just one more creature to feed and care for. Aren't children enough to look after without having a cat that's going to need attention too? When we'd pleaded with Mom, the answer had always been the same, "No cat!" We'd lost all hope.

Then Mom announced that she'd have a surprise for my sister Margaret by Friday. She mentioned some clues, such as that the surprise was fast ...and warm. However, no one—absolutely no one—could have dreamed that it'd be a cat. Then he arrived. Margaret couldn't believe her eyes. She's been marveling ever since. She's unsure to this day what came over her mother to make her change her mind.

Practice M: LABELING STARTERS IN STARTER-VERB QUESTIONS

[From text, page 71]

DIRECTIONS: **Double underline** ALL STARTERS. Imitate the example.

Example: **Does** your neighbor's cat kill birds?

Hasn't this been the coldest spring on record? Can you remember whether the thermometer has reached 90? Isn't it true that the temperature has rarely reached even 80? Haven't we had more rain than usual? Would it be possible that we have had more rainy days than rain-free days? Could the average day-time temperature have been as low as 70? Will this cool weather continue much longer?

Practice N: LABELING STARTERS IN VARIED SENTENCES

[From text, page 71]

DIRECTIONS: **Double underline** the STARTERS in these sentences. Imitate the example.

Example: **Do** bees search for honey on days that **are** overcast?

Shouldn't a dog that must live with a cat be its guardian? If your cat were clawing the rug, wouldn't your watchful dog take action?

Even when they don't face each other, our dog and cat will know what the other is doing. Each day that has passed can't be considered a gain as far as the cat is concerned. Because he didn't bargain on the watchfulness of our dog, he couldn't guess how careful he must now be. Now he won't keep his eyes off the dog when they are in the same room.

Practice P: LABELING STARTERS AND FOLLOWERS

[From text, page 73]

DIRECTIONS: **Double underline** the STARTERS AND FOLLOWERS in these sentences. Imitate the example.

Example: When the sun **is** breaking through mist, the prettiness of the scene **would be** hard to describe.

If you have been doing a lot of daydreaming lately, there may be a reason. You may be doing a lot of growing. You may be experiencing fatigue [*tiredness*]. You could be developing into the real you.

On the other hand, you could have forgotten how necessary sleep is. You could be saying to yourself that TV is more important than sleep. Maybe you have convinced yourself that a novel must be finished before sleep can be allowed. You can shortchange yourself with such beliefs. You must take charge of your life.

Practice Q: FINDING FOLLOWERS WHEN SEPARATED FROM ACCOMPANYING STARTERS

[From text, page 74]

DIRECTIONS: Double underline the STARTERS AND FOLLOWERS in these sentences. Imitate the example.

Example: Though minor league games **are** often **being** played in the town beside ours, we **have** only rarely **been** taking the opportunity to see them.

Our lawn has not been mowed much this spring. The weather has often been the reason. Even when rain was not falling, the grass may still have been wet from earlier rain. It can be dangerous to mow when the grass is slippery.

The weather has not been the only reason. Often our lawn mower is being repaired. First, it was repaired because it just would not start. Then, after it had been used for only a minute, it could no longer be used because a wheel had broken and the ground was being dug up.

Practice R: FINDING STARTERS AND FOLLOWERS

[From text, page 74]

DIRECTIONS: Double underline the STARTERS AND FOLLOWERS in these sentences. Imitate the example.

Example: Though the bird house **was**n't usable, even a mouse **could** once **have been** seen entering it.

1. It is only in the mountains that summer days can be almost cold.
2. What he might have claimed is that he hasn't ever won two races in a row.
3. Whether cars will have become significantly more efficient may depend on many factors.
4. That a car has skidded on this curve can be learned from the nature of the skid marks.
5. Whether typewriters are being replaced by computers can no longer be being debated.
6. An answer that can always be given is that you do not know the answer.
7. Isn't Jack the fellow who was not being allowed to drive?
8. A person can't always be certain that he can't succeed at something until he has at least tried it.
9. Those who have been using ski tows over the years must have gradually been being charged ever higher prices for rides.
10. A swarm of bees that have chosen your house for their home must be immediately informed that they have not been invited.

Practice S: More Finding of Starters and Followers

[From text, page 74]

Directions: **Double underline** the STARTERS AND FOLLOWERS in these sentences. Imitate the example.

Example: If Al **had** looked, he **might have** discovered his error.

1. For dozens of years, every issue of the *Reader's Digest* has been carrying a vocabulary test whose answers are later explained.
2. Since we had been watching the same movie the day before, we sensed that our time could have been being more profitably used.
3. If their antenna could have been placed on a mountain, they would have been reaching at least three more channels.
4. Because our forests are being destroyed, the gypsy moth caterpillars must be stopped.
5. There are some flowers that will not flourish if they have been planted in a shady area.
6. Since Louise would have been being given a second chance unfairly, the teacher was unwilling to agree.
7. Though our electricity has been being cut off for several days, this has never been for more than two hours at a time.
8. Since teachers usually have substitute tests, someone who has been sick would not be being given a test the first day of recovery.

Practice T: Still More Finding of Starters and Followers

[From text, page 74]

Directions: **Double underline** the STARTERS AND FOLLOWERS in these ten sentences.

1. No one who had ever been a winner before was allowed to compete again.
2. According to their plan, all customers can have easily been served within five minutes of their arrival.
3. Billions must be spent on technical assistance and agricultural research before everyone on earth can be properly fed.
4. Though the cost of oil had been leapfrogging, the cost of other goods had not always been increasing as much.
5. Though our skies have been being monitored for decades, our costs may not also be being so carefully watched.
6. "Simple tasks" can become time-consuming burdens if they have not been first thought through.
7. The hay that is now being rustled by the wind can later be fed to cows for their survival.
8. When a movie that the whole family has gathered to watch is not even entertaining, an evening has been wasted that could have been used for some game.
9. A person who is sick begins to realize what it has always meant to be well.
10. When furry creatures have invaded a garage, they must feel that they have somehow been invited.

Practice U: WRITING SENTENCES USING STARTERS AND FOLLOWERS

[From text, page 76]

DIRECTIONS: Write a short sentence FOR EACH OF THESE STARTERS AND FOLLOWERS—***DID, CAN, WAS, BE, BEING, BEEN, HAVE*** **(starter),** and ***HAVE*** **(follower)**. Imitate the example.

Example: I **do** FORM my letters so they can be easily read.

____

____

____

____

____

____

____

____

* * * * *

PARAGRAPH AND ESSAY SUPPLEMENT

CHANGE IN TENSE

GOAL IN THIS MINI-CHAPTER

To change tenses inside a paragraph in the ONLY way permissible—in accompaniment with time-indicator wording.

TIME-INDICATOR WORDING AS TENSE MARKERS

Each of the three "grammatical times" in English—TIME NOW, TIME EARLIER THAN NOW, and TIME LATER THAN NOW—has words in English that MARK the presence of that time. If you EVER want to change tenses (time reference inside a verb) in a paragraph, you MUST USE ONE OF THESE MARKERS (or a similar one)—together with the change in the verb—IN THE SAME SENTENCE.

Here are some examples of these markers:

For TIME NOW: ***now, at this time, at present, currently;***

For TIME EARLIER THAN NOW: ***at that time, ago, yesterday, last ____, in [some time in the past] ;***

For TIME LATER THAN NOW: ***tomorrow, soon, in the future, later, next ____, in [some time in the future] .***

CAUTION

Do not even think of changing tenses inside a paragraph UNLESS YOU ADD A TIME-INDICATOR AS A MARKER AT THE SAME TIME. (The only exception would be a sentence like *He always tells the truth*; this sentence would NOT need an accompanying time marker because it is a general truth in present time—a kind of sentence that must always be written in the present tense.)

PRACTICE V: PLANNING A PRESENT TENSE PARAGRAPH WITH ONE CHANGE

DIRECTIONS: Prepare an outline for a paragraph that starts in the PRESENT TENSE and has ONE AND ONLY ONE TENSE CHANGE **and** accompanying TIME-INDICATOR WORDING. You could write about something that usually takes place—a game; a carnival event; an annual event at school like a play; a town or neighborhood happening; or whatever would be suitable. At the end, you could relate the happenings to something in the past or future. For the "point under discussion," indicate the subject matter of your discussion. Then list the details of what usually takes place, and end with one point that refers to the past or future. Imitate the example outline supplied below.

Example Outline

AN IDEAL BIRTHDAY-PARTY GAME FOR AN 11-YEAR OLD BOY IS A TREASURE HUNT

Out-of-doors
Type of "prize"
Hiding places
Effects: tired and happy
Where the idea came from

Practice W: WRITING A PRESENT TENSE PARAGRAPH WITH ONE CHANGE

DIRECTIONS: Write a paragraph based on the outline you prepared in Practice V. Imitate the example paragraph supplied below. BE SURE TO CHANGE TENSES IN ONE SENTENCE ONLY.

Example Paragraph

AN OUT-OF-DOORS TREASURE HUNT IS THE PERFECT GAME FOR THOSE PARENTS TO CHOOSE WHO CONDUCT BIRTHDAY PARTIES FOR THEIR 11-YEAR OLD SONS. *Boxes of cracker jacks make good "treasures." These fit behind or under rocks; inside, on top of, or behind old trees; and inside dilapidated stone walls. The searching lads run here and there and quickly tire themselves out. They end the day happy and ready to go home. Friends of ours* ***dreamed*** *this game up* ***LAST YEAR*** *when their oldest boy* ***turned*** *eleven.* [Notice how the wording *last year* allowed the writer to use the two past-tense verbs *dreamed* and *turned*.]

Practice X: Planning a Past Tense Paragraph with One Change

Directions: Prepare an outline for a paragraph that starts in the past tense and includes one tense change (together with its accompanying time-indicator wording). You could write about something that happened to you (or to someone you know) that would be interesting and could have some humor or some lesson to teach. End the story by stating the lesson as a general truth, making a prediction about the future, or explaining what the situation is now. For the "point under discussion," indicate the subject matter of your discussion. Then list the details of what took place, and end with one point that refers to the past or future. Imitate the example outline supplied below.

Example Outline

Son and friends went camping on nearby hill

Had equipment needed
Ran out of food so returned
Saw bear in path
Ran
Stayed home that night
Happy to do day-time "camping" now

Practice Y: Writing a Past Tense Paragraph with One Change

Directions: Write a paragraph based on the outline you prepared in Practice X. Imitate the example paragraph supplied below. Be sure to change tenses in one sentence only.

Example Paragraph

My son and a friend decided to camp out on a nearby hill one night. They brought their lantern and all their belongings to their favorite spot. After a few hours they got hungry so they headed back to the house. But something else was in the woods. A brown bear came along to see what was making all the noise. When the boys saw him, they dropped the lantern and raced down the mountainside. Needless to say, they "camped" inside the house that night. ***Now*** *they* ***prefer*** *to do their "camping" in the daytime.* [Notice how the word *now* allowed the writer to switch to the present tense.]

Chapter 6

Helping Verbs as Markers of Main Verbs

Practice A: LABELING *WHAT*-ANSWERING WORDS IN SHORTER SENTENCES

[From text, page 85]

DIRECTIONS: For each sentence, first label each starter and follower. Then say all the words of the sentence through the last helper in the set and ask *WHAT*. For now only, place a small circle under it. Imitate the example.

Example: The candy is being evenly divided among the children.

1. We have broken several records.
2. Teachers have many approaches.
3. Samples may be being sent to everyone in our area.
4. Sue didn't even take notes on the material. [Say *didn't WHAT?*]
5. Hal should be being allowed to wrestle.
6. A fluorescent lamp should furnish a more even light.
7. She would have then begun her project.
8. Jane doesn't often take breaks even for a snack. [Say *doesn't WHAT?*]
9. Ed has long been unsure of his goals in life.
10. Our supply of paper should soon be arriving.
11. Carl could have been easily mistaken for me.
12. Sharon might even come sooner than that.

Practice B: LABELING *WHAT*-ANSWERING WORDS IN LONGER SENTENCES

[From text, page 85]

DIRECTIONS: For each sentence, first label each starter and follower. Then say all the words of the sentence through each last helper in the set and ask *WHAT*. For now only, place a small circle under it. Imitate the example.

Example: Since a Baltimore oriole has a bright orange color, even nearsighted people will have occasionally seen one.

1. Few who are trustworthy would consider cheating on a test.
2. Since he had his motorcycle accident, Jim has been being given whirlpool treatments.
3. Our supply of paper should be arriving soon because we were promised that it would take no more than two weeks.
4. The town that I am now in [the words *now* and *in* do not answer *WHAT*—they answer *WHEN* and *WHERE* respectively] was scarcely touched by a recent snowstorm that had blanketed nearby areas with up to two feet of snow.
5. After the missionary had learned the language, he was more fully accepted by the natives.
6. After the electrical field men left their job, the wires that they had been working on were crackling and a fire was starting.
7. When the votes were finally counted, each officer had received a clear majority.
8. The "palettes," or platforms, that heavy material is shipped on can have many uses around a farm.
9. Anyone could know that something special was being arranged because tables were being repositioned and everyone was hurrying about.
10. Although you can find many good vacuum cleaners on the market, only some brands have a reputation for being ones that will last for a long time.

Practice C: LABELING *WHAT*-ANSWERING WORDS IN SENTENCES WITH *NOT*

[From text page 86]

DIRECTIONS: For these sentences, **first** double underline all starters and followers. **Second**, rewrite as a **contraction** all the starter-plus-*not* combinations that you can. **Third**, say all the words of the sentence through each last helper (to include appropriate starter plus *n't* contractions) in the set and ask *WHAT*. For now only, place a small circle under the word that answers *WHAT*. Imitate the example.

Examples:

[wouldn't]
The stapler <u>would</u> ^ not work because several staples <u>had</u> somehow jammed.

[won't]
The mailman <u>will</u> ^ not <u>be</u> arriving early if it <u>is</u> the day after a holiday.

1. Snowmobiles are not so popular anymore.

2. We do not know what the future will bring.

3. Birds do not fly about in severe storms.

4. You should not place a hot pan on an unprotected surface.

5. Chairs that are left out-of-doors do not always last.

6. Anything mechanical that is stuck should not be forced to work.

7. They have not once changed their plan.

8. The top-heavy old pine tree could not withstand the powerful gust of wind.

9. The window was not open more than an inch.

10. A store owner must not forget to lock his store.

Practice D: More Labeling of *What*-answering Words in Sentences With *Not*

[From text, page 86]

Directions: For these sentences, **first** double underline all starters and followers. **Second**, rewrite as a **contraction** all the starter-plus-*not* combinations that you can. **Third**, say all the words of the sentence through each last helper (to include appropriate starter plus *n't* contractions) in the set and ask *WHAT*. For now only, place a small circle under the word that answers *WHAT*. Imitate the example in Practice C.

1. If it had not rained all afternoon, we could have played baseball.

2. Though the sun had been out all morning, the air was not very clear.

3. Since we had no flour, my sister couldn't finish the cookies she had started.

4. Though college is expensive, it is not an opportunity to be lightly disregarded.

5. When a house is on a sharp curve [*on a sharp curve* answers *WHERE*], the owners should not create additional hazards for motorists.

6. Though the wind had died down, the heat was not as unbearable as it could have been.

7. When our dog is chasing a car, he is not so careless that he does not respect its wheels.

8. When a cat is prowling, it cannot be easily heard.

Practice E: LABELING VERBS USING TEST 1 THROUGH PART C, STEP 1—ADDING *ING*

[From text, page 89]

DIRECTIONS: For these expressions, first label all starters and followers. Then find the *WHAT*-answering word. Thirdly, test whether you can add *ing*—**outside the expression** (but testing in your head). If you can add *ing*, double underline the word. If you cannot add *ing*, place a check under the word. Imitate the example.

Examples: should have a leader ✓   will ^[won't] not quickly complain

1. is wider
2. has a few fears
3. would easily determine
4. will be an opener
5. does not consider
6. will be much participation
7. has some courage
8. should not even plan
9. can be too destructive
10. were not expensive
11. will soon settle
12. may have a problem

Practice F: LABELING VERBS USING TEST 1 THROUGH PART C, STEP 1—ADDING *ING*

[From text, page 89]

DIRECTIONS: For these expressions, first label all starters and followers. Then find the *WHAT*-answering word. Third, test whether you can add *ing*—**outside the expression** (but testing in your head). If you can add *ing*, double underline the word. If you can not add *ing*, place a check under the word. Imitate the example in Practice E.

1. has acceptable manners
2. is the owner
3. might later own
4. were reasonable
5. would be somewhat certain
6. would not decide
7. should not now erase
8. might have answers
9. could then remain
10. may even double
11. am unsure
12. had no permission

Practice G: LABELING VERBS USING TEST 1 THROUGH PART C, STEP 1—ADDING *ING*

[From text, page 89]

DIRECTIONS: For these sentences, first label all starters and followers. Then find the *WHAT*-answering word. Third, test whether you can add *ing*—**outside the sentence** (but testing in your head). If you can add *ing*, double underline the word. If you cannot add *ing*, place a check under the word. Imitate the example.

Example: No one who has been personally hurt in a serious car accident could ever deny that a seat belt is important. ✓

1. Few who would like to ski regularly can easily afford it.
2. If you were a member of my household, you would not quickly get your hands on the *Reader's Digest* when it has just come in the mail.
3. If a family has three baby-sitters on call, arguments will eventually arise over the jobs that will be available.
4. When a family has a dog around, they can feel less guilty if they don't quite finish all that is on their plates. [The wording *on their plates* answers *WHERE*.]

Practice H: LABELING VERBS USING TEST 1 THROUGH PART C, STEP 1—ADDING *ING*

[From text, page 89]

DIRECTIONS: For the sentences in this passage, first label all starters and followers. Then find the *WHAT*-answering word. Thirdly, test whether you can add *ing*—**outside the sentence** (but testing in your head). If you can add *ing*, double underline the word. If you can not add *ing*, place a check under the word. Imitate the example in Practice G.

Wind

When I was much younger, I would scarcely pay attention to the wind. I don't remember a single windstorm, blizzard, or hurricane.

Now, however, I am someone who lives in the country. My home is in the mountains and on a hillside [there is no *WHAT*-answering word after *is* here]. This home is prey [*victim*] to winds that can hurl themselves against it from the north and from the south. This is comparable to a house that might sit in the middle of a wind tunnel.

Practice J: Labeling Verbs Using Test 1 Through Part C, Step 2—*Ed* Exception

[From text, page 90]

Directions: For these expressions, first label all starters and followers. **Second**, find the *WHAT*-answering word. **Third**, test *ed* words by substituting *ing*—**outside the sentence**; otherwise, test the word by just adding *ing*. If the word is a verb, double underline it. If it is not, place a check under it. Imitate the example.

Example: are being duly certified   [can't] ^ can not have been untouched ✓

1.	could not have argued	11.	will be soon revived
2.	had somehow determined	12.	has not yet answered
3.	was not that crooked	13.	had not been mobile
4.	could not be certain	14.	was not that wicked
5.	has not already dissolved	15.	are being approached
6.	were now undecided	16.	could then prevent
7.	are seldom contained	17.	will be undefeated
8.	have sometimes improved	18.	is unusually worried
9.	is dogged	19.	is rather jagged
10.	can be easily reopened	20.	might have then ruined

Practice K: LABELING VERBS USING TEST 1 THROUGH PART C, STEP 2—*ED* EXCEPTION

[From text, page 90]

DIRECTIONS: For these sentences, first label all starters and followers. **Second**, find the *WHAT*-answering word. **Third**, test *ed* words by substituting *ing*—**outside the sentence**; otherwise, test the word by just adding *ing*. If the word is a verb, double underline it. If it is not, place a check under it. Imitate the example.

Example: If your work is unfinished, your effort has been incomplete.
✓ ✓

1. Since the paper had edges that were ragged, it was unusable.

2. When a door can't be closed easily, its latch should be examined.

3. The services that are expected of parents are often unappreciated by their children.

4. Since the wind has unexpected gusts, the windchill factor is unpredictable.

5. If a coffee pot is thoughtlessly plugged into the same outlet as a waffle iron, a person could easily blow a fuse.

6. Once a child was electrocuted because his parents had not considered the importance of unplugging the toaster.

7. If you have a warped tennis racket, you have been careless with it.

8. The compliment was not undeserved; it was overdue.

Practice L: LABELING VERBS USING TEST 1 THROUGH PART C, STEP 2—*ING* EXCEPTION

[From text, page 91]

DIRECTIONS: For these expressions, **first** label all starters and followers. **Second**, find the *WHAT*-answering word. **Third**, test *ing* words by dropping *ing*, and test *ed* words by substituting *ing*; otherwise, test the word by just adding *ing*. If the word is a verb, double underline it. If it is not, place a check under it. Imitate the example.

Example: will be soon planning   was unfilling ✓

1. should soon be decreasing
2. is now arguing
3. was sometimes unflattering
4. could be unending
5. has been recently deafening
6. would not be unfailing
7. are not relabeling
8. may not be undeserving
9. should be complimenting
10. could have been bossing
11. is suddenly forcing
12. has been long undecided
13. were somewhat uncaring
14. is now debating
15. could not have then been omitted
16. will not be unwilling
17. should have been arriving
18. might be too jagged
19. has been lately underestimating
20. shouldn't be now retracing

Practice M: Labeling Verbs Using Test 1 through Part C, Step 2—*Ing* Exception

[From text, page 91]

Directions: For these expressions, **first** label all starters and followers. **Second**, find the *WHAT*-answering word. **Third**, test *ing* words by dropping *ing*, and test *ed* words by substituting *ing*; otherwise, test the word by just adding *ing*. If the word is a verb, double underline it. If it is not, place a check under it. Imitate the example.

Example: Since his loyalty is unswerving, he should be receiving a higher salary.
✓

1. Nothing has been working as well as we were once planning.
2. When the engine was racing, the belt would loosen.
3. The water was untempting, and the clouds were unyielding.
4. All were singing, but few were harmonizing.
5. Since people were not complaining, the air conditioner was never repaired.
6. The driver had been so distracted that he had turned left when he should have been turning right.
7. A few were talking at the top of their voices beneath the window where I was unsuccessfully trying to sleep.
8. If you are hurrying, it is likely that you are being unnecessarily careless.

Practice N: Supplying the Basic Spelling for Verbs in Their After-Had Spelling

[From text, page 92]

Directions: In the blank spaces to the right of each word, supply the correct basic spelling for the verb. An easy method to find the basic spelling is to try to say the word with *will* in front of it. The spelling that accompanies *will* is always the basic spelling. Imitate the examples.

Examples: broken __break__ [*will break*] gone __go__ [*will go*]

arisen __________	broken __________	dealt __________
beaten __________	brought __________	done __________
begun __________	built __________	drawn __________
bent __________	bought __________	driven __________
bitten __________	caught __________	drunk __________
blown __________	chosen __________	dug __________
borne __________	clung __________	eaten __________
bound __________	crept __________	fallen __________

Practice P: SUPPLYING THE BASIC SPELLING FOR VERBS IN THEIR AFTER-HAD SPELLING

[From text, page 92]

DIRECTIONS: In the blank spaces to the right of each word, supply the correct basic spelling for the verb. An easy method to find the basic spelling is to try to say the word with *will* in front of it. Imitate the examples in Practice N.

fed ________	frozen ________	kept ________
fled ________	given ________	known ________
flung ________	gone ________	laid ________
flown ________	gotten ________	lain ________
forbidden ________	grown ________	led ________
forgotten ________	hidden ________	left ________
fought ________	held ________	lent ________
found ________	hung ________	lit ________

Practice Q: SUPPLYING THE BASIC SPELLING FOR VERBS IN THEIR AFTER-HAD SPELLING

[From text, page 92]

DIRECTIONS: In the blank spaces to the right of each word, supply the correct basic spelling for the verb. An easy method to find the basic spelling is to try to say the word with *will* in front of it. Imitate the examples in Practice N.

lost ________	said ________	slain ________
made ________	seen ________	slung ________
meant ________	sewn ________	sold ________
paid ________	sat ________	sought ________
proven ________	shaken ________	spent ________
ridden ________	shone ________	spoken ________
risen ________	shown ________	sprung ________
rung ________	shrunk ________	spun ________

Practice R: Supplying the Basic Spelling for Verbs in Their After-Had Spelling

[From text, page 92]

Directions: In the blank spaces to the right of each word, supply the correct basic spelling for the verb. An easy method to find the basic spelling is to try to say the word with *will* in front of it. Imitate the examples in Practice N.

stolen ________	sunk ________	thought ________
stood ________	swollen ________	torn ________
striven ________	sworn ________	thrown ________
struck ________	swum ________	worn ________
stung ________	swung ________	written ________
stunk ________	taken ________	wrung ________
sung ________	taught ________	

Practice S: Labeling Verbs Using Test 1 through Part C, Step 2—Irregular Verb Exception

[From text, page 92]

Directions: For these expressions, **first** label all starters and followers. **Second**, find the *WHAT*-answering word. **Third**, test *ing* words by dropping *ing*; test *ed* words by substituting *ing*; **RECOGNIZE** IRREGULAR VERBS in their past tense; otherwise, test the word by just adding *ing*. If the word is a verb, double underline it. If it is not, place a check under it. Imitate the example.

Example: had been wrung dry   shouldn't have spoken so quickly

1. was well spent
2. should then have stood
3. had been too quickly given
4. could have new scissors
5. was not even chosen
6. may have later brought
7. are being easily bent
8. will be later spoken to
9. has gone for a walk
10. may have understandably disapproved

Practice T: Labeling Verbs Using Test 1 through Part C, Step 2—Irregular Verb Exception

[From text, page 93]

Directions: For these sentences, **first** label all starters and followers. **Second**, find the *WHAT*-answering word. **Third**, test *ing* words by dropping *ing*; test *ed* words by substituting *ing*; **RECOGNIZE** IRREGULAR VERBS in their past tense; otherwise, test the word by just adding *ing*. If the word is a verb, double underline it. If it is not, place a check under it. Imitate the example.

Example: Though none of the plates has ever been broken, many have lost some color because the water has been so hot.
✓

1. If my father had left earlier, he would not have had to hurry.
2. Though Pedro had stood beside a bee's nest, he was not stung.
3. If Andrew had not flung his racket at the net, he might have given the impression of being a better sport.
4. After Maria had torn the sleeve of her favorite blouse, her eyes were swollen with tears.
5. The candy that was forbidden was not easily forgotten by the mouth-watering children.
6. The clock that was thrown out because it had been struck by lightning had been bought only a short while before.

Practice U: Labeling Verbs Using Test 1 through Part C, Step 2—Irregular Verb Exception

[From text, page 93]

Directions: For these sentences, follow the directions given in Practice T.

1. If Bruce had only said that he had seen the sign, we could have gotten to our destination much sooner.
2. Though the temperature had fallen, the air had not lost its fragrance and everyone was still being bitten by mosquitoes.
3. If the wind had not blown down the tree, the electricity wouldn't have been cut off for an hour.
4. Though Tom's mother had lain down for a rest, she was keeping an ear open to hear the phone and was sure to answer it if it should ring.
5. Though Alice had brought her umbrella, she had ridden all the way to school before she remembered her rubbers.
6. Though Barb was not uncaring, she was caught in a dilemma between what was desirable and what was possible.

Practice V: Labeling Verbs Using Test 1 through Part C, Step 3

[From text, page 94]

Directions: For these sentences, **first** label all starters and followers. **Second**, find the *WHAT*-answering word. **Third**, test *ing* words by dropping *ing*; test *ed* words by substituting *ing*; recognize irregular verbs in their past tense; otherwise, test the word by just adding *ing*. If the dictionary meaning also stays the same, label the word a verb. If not, place a check under it. Imitate the example.

Example: All who have common sense will quickly say no to addictive drugs.
✓

1. No one who has a heavy schedule has time for much TV.
2. A few of us will be free this afternoon.
3. Children who are mean to others sometimes have an unhappy home.
4. Though Dave has room for improvement as an organizer, he can do remarkably well with limited resources despite this.
5. The flowers were pretty though there could have been more.
6 Students are usually open to good suggestions from an upperclassman who is kind enough to offer them.

Practice W: Labeling Verbs Using Test 1 through Part C, Step 3

[From text, page 94]

Directions: For these sentences, **first** label all starters and followers. **Second**, find the *WHAT*-answering word. **Third**, test *ing* words by dropping *ing*; test *ed* words by substituting *ing*; recognize irregular verbs in their past tense; otherwise, test the word by just adding *ing*. If the dictionary meaning also stays the same, label the word a verb. If not, place a check under it. Imitate the example in Practice V.

1. The increase in amount of rain was noticeable at first because there were floods in some areas.
2. My brother has concern for one of his children who can not see well.
3. Though the parts have been ready for a long time, the mechanic could not get free enough to tackle the job.
4. When a stored jar is open so its contents can have been contaminated, the owner must be wary.

Practice X: LABELING VERBS USING TEST 1—STEPS 1, 2, AND 3

[From text, page 96]

DIRECTIONS: For this passage, carry out Test 1 in full.

Profiting from Class Time

The question has come up as to whether it is possible for students to stay alert throughout a class hour. There is at least one person who is sure that this can be achieved, but he would insist that the several strategies available must be chosen according to the type of classroom activity in progress.

You must remember that a classroom hour is only sometimes being devoted to explanation alone. Occasionally, a student will ask a question; or a student may be being asked a question by the teacher. Other times discussions are the activity during which a student must be staying alert.

There are several strategies that you can use. The chief one, because it is the strategy that students should use while the teacher is speaking, would be this: you should have a racing pen. If students are eager to keep alert, they must be prepared to jot onto paper everything that their teachers might say—even though they may be so enjoying the teacher that they would rather be being simply entertained by what is being said.

Unfortunately, that strategy will not be helpful when questions are being asked. In order to stay on top of questions, you could pretend that the instructor will always be calling on you first. Then you will always be ready with an answer. If you are smart, your answer can then be compared to any answer given as a double check.

As you may have by now guessed, the "racing pen" strategy will not be too helpful during discussion time either. This is because the give-and-take of discussions is usually too fast for this. During discussions, it would be better for students to participate and mentally keep track of what is said.

PARAGRAPH AND ESSAY SUPPLEMENT

GIVING DIRECTIONS

GOAL IN THIS MINI-CHAPTER

To practice providing others with unmistakably clear directions for getting from one place to another.

PRACTICE Y: PLANNING DIRECTIONS FOR GETTING SOMEPLACE ON FOOT

DIRECTIONS: Prepare an outline for a paragraph explaining clearly how to get from one place (any place) to another ON FOOT. You might give directions from where you live to the school; from where you live to the grocery store; or from where you live to a friend's house. There must be at least FIVE change-of-direction locations along the way. In your direction giving, be sure to include clear-cut indicators as to where to turn, the degree (angle) of the turn, and the approximate distance(s) to travel from one change-of-direction point to another. Do not forget to tell the reader which way to turn at the end of the walkway or driveway where you live. Also include all the clues needed to know that the right destination has been reached. In your "point to be discussed," indicate that you are giving directions and from where to where. Then list the details of the steps that the reader must follow to be successful. Imitate the example outline supplied here.

Example Outline

THE WALK FROM MY PLACE TO ED'S

Go right at end of driveway.
Take 1st right (after one house) onto Division St.
Take next right (at "T") onto Main St.
Take next left (at light) onto Kingston St. (Rte. 28).
Take 2nd left off of Kingston St. (after a bridge and immediately after a 90 degree right-hand curve in the road)—note wide opening—onto Sheldon Dr.
Take 1st left (up a hill and about 1/10 of a mile) onto Park Pl.
Go to 3rd house on right, a brown one, #8 (Park Place).

Practice Z: WRITING DIRECTIONS FOR GETTING SOMEPLACE ON FOOT

DIRECTIONS: Write a paragraph based on the outline you prepared in Practice Y. Imitate the example paragraph supplied below

Example Paragraph

IT IS ABOUT A THREE-QUARTERS OF A MILE WALK FROM MY HOUSE TO ED STANLEY'S. *When you leave our driveway, you go to the right past the first house and turn right at the road there, which is Division Street. Walk down Division Street one block to the "T" at Main Street and go right. Walk one block again to the light and go left on Kingston Street (also called Rte. 28), which goes west out of town toward Andes. Walk down Kingston Street about 1/8 of a mile over a bridge, past the first left turn, and around a 90 degree turn—then take an immediate left turn onto Sheldon Drive (you cannot miss it because it is at one of the entrances to the school and is at least three roadways wide at that intersection). Bear left up a steep hill about 1/10 of a mile, and take your first left onto Park Place. Ed's house is the third on the right-hand side. It is a brown house with a wide, fairly steep, and short driveway on the right of the house; he lives at 8 Park Place.*

Practice AA: PLANNING AND WRITING OUT DIRECTIONS FOR GETTING SOMEPLACE BY CAR

DIRECTIONS: Follow the directions and imitate the example outline and paragraph for Practices Y and Z, but tell the reader how to get from one place (any place) to another BY CAR. If you are not a driver, choose a local route that you know from walking if you can—but with cues that will help a driver. Otherwise, give another route for on-foot travel from the one used for Practice Z but one that is more challenging.

Chapter 7

Finding Remaining Main Verbs

Practice A: ADDING THE *DID* SUBSTITUTION TO SINGLE WORDS

[From text, page 113]

DIRECTIONS: **WRITE OUT THE *DID* SUBSTITUTE SPELLING** for each of these words. All answers must have **two words**. Place a check under those that can **never** be a verb.

Example: proved _did prove_

wicked _did wick_
✓

laughed ________________

unedited ________________

opened ________________

crooked ________________

tracked ________________

entered ________________

tired ________________

inched ________________

unneeded ________________

unindented ________________

Practice B: APPLYING THREE SPELLING TIPS

[From text, page 115]

DIRECTIONS: Add *DID* to these words, and **WRITE OUT THE WHOLE *DID* SUBSTITUTE SPELLING**. **Two words** are required. Imitate the example.

Example: carried _did carry_ occurred _did occur_

planned ________________

hurried ________________

closed ________________

emptied ________________

fined ________________

raced ________________

preferred ________________

surfaced ________________

married ________________

omitted ________________

Practice C: ADDING THE *DID* SUBSTITUTION INSIDE SENTENCES WITH ONE *ED* WORD

[From text, page 116]

DIRECTIONS: **WRITE OUT CORRECTLY THE *DID* SUBSTITUTE SPELLING** for the words in these sentences THAT END IN ***ED***. Double underline words that are verbs, and place a check under words that are not verbs. Imitate the examples.

Important Note: For these practices, use the *do, does,* or *did* substitution only for the word you are testing. In other words, use the original wording (**not** substitutions) for all wording earlier than the word that you are now testing.

Note Also: Do **not** be surprised if the result is NONSENSE instead of English. The fact that the result is nonsense is part of the proof that the word is not a verb and must, therefore, receive a check mark.

[did tame]
Example A: A ^ tamed skunk prowls without fear.
✓

[did charm]
Example B: Her flashing smile ^ charmed the listener.

1. Everyone knew that the undefeated team was not invincible.

2. The scavenger found a discarded cigar box.

3. When Al slipped from his skateboard, he broke his arm.

4. The frozen fish tasted good even weeks later.

5. Satisfying pastimes brought my retired father much happiness.

6. Despite the choppy water, the boat stayed dry.

7. The soda bought the night before lasted the whole time.

8. Unfortunately, established rules sometimes need reevaluation.

9. Everything went wrong with the pretested appliance.

10. The envelopes in the basement became glued from the humidity.

Practice D: ADDING THE *DID* SUBSTITUTION INSIDE SENTENCES WITH EXTRA *ED* WORDS

[From text, page 116]

DIRECTIONS: Carry out the same directions as for Practice C but EXPECT MORE THAN ONE ***ED*** WORD in a sentence. Imitate the example.

[did worry] **[did need]**

Example: The ^ worried ✓ businessman ^ needed more time.

1. He continued at an unhurried pace.

2. The weakened climbers wanted to rest.

3. The disorganized boy tidied his room only when so inclined.

4. The car hesitated at first but then proceeded on.

5. It never occurred to him that the stalled car needed gas.

6. The exhausted jogger refused to quit.

Practice E: ADDING THE *DID* SUBSTITUTION AFTER CARRYING OUT THE HELPERS PLUS WHAT/ING WORD VERB TEST

[From text, page 116]

DIRECTIONS: For these sentences, use **both** verb tests. **First**, FIND ALL VERBS BY THE HELPERS PLUS WHAT/ING WORD VERB TEST. **Second,** WRITE OUT THE *DID* SUBSTITUTE SPELLING BUT ONLY FOR ***UNLABELED ED* WORDS**. **Then** double underline words that are verbs, and place a check under words that are not verbs. Imitate the example.

Example: Since Jim ^ [**did want**] wanted a ^ [**did furnish**] furnished ✓ apartment, he had studied the ads for one that he would like.

1. After he planned his day and finished his chores, Jerry would ride his bike to some predetermined activity.

2. Because the thistle had not been destroyed before its seeds had spread, fresh and undesired thistles appeared everywhere.

3. The doctor parked his car where he could get out easily if called for an emergency.

4. The view that Beverly could see from her window rested her tired eyes whenever she looked up.

5. Because the weeds that he had pulled from his garden were left between the rows, they enriched the farmer's large garden.

Practice F: ADDING THE *DOES* OR *DO* SUBSTITUTION TO SINGLE WORDS

[From text, page 117]

DIRECTIONS: **WRITE OUT THE *DOES* OR *DO* SUBSTITUTE SPELLING** for each of these words. All answers must have **two words**. Do **not** be surprised if the result is nonsense instead of English. The fact that the result is nonsense is part of the proof that the word is not a verb. Imitate the examples.

Examples: glass **do glass** raises **does raise**

progresses **does progress** guess **do guess**

loses ________________ losses ________________

mess ________________ possess ________________

waters ________________ always ________________

less ________________ trudges ________________

sometimes ________________ stress ________________

Practice G: APPLYING TWO SPELLING TIPS

[From text, page 118]

DIRECTIONS: **WRITE OUT THE *DOES* OR *DO* SUBSTITUTE SPELLING** for each of these words (keep in mind the spelling tips). All answers must have **two words.** Imitate the examples. Do **not** be surprised if the result is NONSENSE instead of English. The fact that the result is nonsense is part of the proof that the word is not a verb. Imitate the example.

Example: pretties **does pretty** lad's **do lad's**

worries ________________ certifies ________________

cities ________________ pantries ________________

owner's ________________ country's ________________

shelves ________________ tries ________________

believes ________________ child's ________________

Practice H: ADDING THE *DOES* OR *DO* SUBSTITUTION INSIDE SENTENCES FOR JUST *S/ES* WORDS

[From text, page 119]

DIRECTIONS: For all the WORDS THAT END IN ***S/ES*** in these sentences, WRITE OUT THE *DOES* OR *DO* SUBSTITUTE SPELLING (keep the spelling tips in mind). Double underline words that are verbs, and place a check under words that are not verbs. Imitate the example.

Example: Ripe ^ **[does cherry]** cherries ✓ glisten in the ^ **[do sun's]** sun's ✓ ^ **[does ray]** rays ✓.

1. Each trip to town uses more gas.

2. When Warren borrows his sister's tennis racket, he plays better.

3. Though Danielle tries her best, she lacks her brother's stamina.

4. Some snakes hiss at their molesters.

5. Cheerful givers win people's hearts.

6. The fries and sodas cost more at Pete's.

Practice J: ADDING THE *DOES*, *DID* OR *DO* SUBSTITUTION INSIDE SENTENCES WITH BOTH *S/ES* AND *ED* WORDS

[From text, page 119]

DIRECTIONS: For all WORDS THAT END IN ***S/ES*** OR ***ED***—OR ARE **IRREGULAR VERBS** IN THEIR PAST TENSE SPELLING—in these sentences, **write out the *does, do,* or *did* substitute spelling**. Then place a double underline under words that are verbs and a check under words that are not verbs. Imitate the example.

Example: Sometimes a lesson ^ **[did learn]** learned ✓ the hard way ^ **[does benefit]** <u>benefits</u> the learner immeasurably.

1. The landlord's declared reasons satisfied none of the tenants.

2. A tossed stone skips and bounces over water when propelled right.

3. Everyone hates cluttered roads and endless lines at bridges.

4. A delayed payment means increased debts.

5. Excessive stress sometimes causes heightened blood pressure.

Practice K: Adding the *Does, Did* or *Do* Substitution after Carrying out the Helpers plus *What/Ing* Word Verb Test

[From text, page 119]

Directions: For these sentences, use both verb tests. **First,** FIND ALL VERBS BY THE HELPERS PLUS WHAT/ING WORD VERB TEST. **Second,** WRITE OUT THE *DO, DID* OR *DOES* SUBSTITUTE SPELLING—FOR ***S/ES*** AND ***ED*** WORDS AND **IRREGULAR VERBS** IN THEIR PAST TENSE—**but only for unlabeled words**. **Then** double underline words that are verbs, and place a check under words that are not verbs.

1. The bubbles that a mountain brook forms are often filled with air.
2. Divided highways have proven safer because there is less danger of an unexpected collision.
3. The rewarded dog wagged his tail and settled at his master's feet.
4. Sometimes families that have lived without TV for a few months no longer wish so eagerly that their parents would get it fixed.
5. A whole day of rain could scarcely be sandwiched between two days spoiled by scarcely a cloud.
6. Trees harmed by heavy winds will grow up crooked but proud.

Practice L: Supplying the Basic Spelling for Irregular Verbs in Their Past Tense

[From text, page 120]

Directions: In the blank spaces to the right of each word, supply the **correct basic spelling** for that verb. If you say the word in a sentence with *DID*, you will come up with the right spelling. Imitate the example.

Example: broke __**break**__ saw __**see**__

arose ________	bid ________	built ________	came ________
ate ________	bit ________	burnt ________	caught ________
awoke ________	bled ________	bound ________	chose ________
became ________	blew ________	bred ________	clung ________
began ________	bore ________	broke ________	crept ________
bent ________	bought ________	brought ________	dealt ________

Practice M: Supplying the Basic Spelling for Irregular Verbs in Their Past Tense

[From text, page 120]

Directions: In the blank spaces to the right of each word, supply the **correct basic spelling** for that verb. If you say the word in a sentence with *DID*, you will come up with the right spelling. Imitate the example in Practice L.

did ____________

dove ____________

drank ____________

dreamt ____________

drew ____________

drove ____________

dug ____________

dwelt ____________

fed ____________

fell ____________

fled ____________

flew ____________

flung ____________

forbade ____________

forgot ____________

fought ____________

found ____________

froze ____________

gave ____________

got ____________

grew ____________

held ____________

hid ____________

hung ____________

kept ____________

knew ____________

laid ____________

Practice N: Supplying the Basic Spelling for Irregular Verbs in Their Past Tense

[From text, page 120]

Directions: In the blank spaces to the right of each word, supply the **correct basic spelling** for that verb. If you say the word in a sentence with *DID*, you will come up with the right spelling. Imitate the example in Practice L.

lay ____________

leapt ____________

led ____________

left ____________

lent ____________

lit ____________

lost ____________

made ____________

meant ____________

paid ____________

ran ____________

rang ____________

read ____________

rid ____________

rode ____________

rose ____________

said ____________

sang ____________

sank ____________

saw ____________

shook ____________

shone ____________

shrank ____________

slew ____________

slung ____________

sold ____________

Practice P: SUPPLYING THE BASIC SPELLING FOR IRREGULAR VERBS IN THEIR PAST TENSE

[From text, page 120]

DIRECTIONS: In the blank spaces to the right of each word, supply the **correct basic spelling** for that verb. If you say the word in a sentence with *DID*, you will arrive at the right spelling. Imitate the examples in Practice L.

sought ________	strove ________	threw ________
spent ________	struck ________	took ________
spoke ________	strung ________	tore ________
sprang ________	stung ________	went ________
spun ________	swam ________	woke ________
stank ________	swore ________	wore ________
stole ________	taught ________	wrote ________
stood ________	thought ________	wrung ________

Practice Q: ADDING THE *DID* SUBSTITUTION INSIDE SENTENCES FOR JUST IRREGULAR VERBS IN THEIR PAST TENSE

[From text, page 120]

DIRECTIONS: For these sentences, WRITE OUT CORRECTLY THE *DID* SUBSTITUTE SPELLING FOR **ALL IRREGULAR VERBS** that carry past tense. Double underline words that are verbs. Imitate the example.

[did swim] [did eat]
Example: After we ^ swam, we ^ ate dinner.

1. The branch fell into the fire; the ants fled.

2. The students knew the material after the teacher taught it.

3. I wrote that after I lost in the finals.

4. We spoke about a lot of things as we went to the game.

5. After we took the finals, we sought relaxation.

6. The sun shone, and the plants grew.

Practice R: ADDING THE *DOES, DID* OR *DO* SUBSTITUTION INSIDE SENTENCES WITH *S/ES* AND *ED* WORDS AND IRREGULAR VERBS IN THEIR PAST TENSE

[From text, page 120]

DIRECTIONS: For all words that end in ***S/ES*** or ***ED*** or are **IRREGULAR VERBS** (in their past tense) in these sentences, WRITE OUT THE *DOES, DO,* OR *DID* SUBSTITUTE SPELLING. Then double underline words that are verbs, and place a check under words that are not verbs. Imitate the example.

Example: The ^ **[did break]** broken ✓ limb ^ **[did hang]** hung limply from the tree for ^ **[does hour]** hours ✓ after Frank ^ **[did try]** tried to swing from it.

1. A toy damaged by one child makes a perfect gift for another.

2. My father won by more votes than he expected.

3. The entries Walt sent surprised his mother and pleased his father.

4. The clock disassembled by Ken needs more skillful hands than his if to be rebuilt.

5. When the fish Sam caught got away, the lesson taught remained.

6. The stress that this job demands causes unusual tiredness and heightened emotions.

Practice S: ADDING THE *DOES*, *DID* OR *DO* SUBSTITUTION AFTER CARRYING OUT THE HELPERS PLUS WHAT/ING WORD VERB TEST

[From text, page 120]

DIRECTIONS: For these sentences, use BOTH verb tests. **First,** FIND ALL VERBS BY THE HELPERS PLUS WHAT/ING WORD VERB TEST. **Second,** WRITE OUT THE *DO, DID,* OR *DOES* SUBSTITUTE SPELLING—FOR ***S/ES*** AND ***ED*** WORDS AND **IRREGULAR VERBS** in their past tense—**but only for UNlabeled words**. **Then** double underline all verbs, and place a check under all words that are not verbs.

1. After he heard that he had passed the test , Pat went wild with excitement.

2. If anyone should select an already bought item, he is quickly told by the undistracted manager.

3. The pen that Warren borrowed for the unexpected quiz fell and broke before he could return it.

4. An allowance that is given weekly could last less than a day for the youth who takes half-hearted precautions.

5. When lightning struck two nearby trees, light and heavy sleepers alike awoke immediately.

6. A calendar that lacks space for jottings is not worth what it cost.

Practice T: ADDING THE *DO* SUBSTITUTION TO SINGLE WORDS

[From text, page 121]

DIRECTIONS: WRITE OUT THE ***DO*** SUBSTITUTE SPELLING for each of these words. All answers must have **two words**. Imitate the examples. Do **not** be surprised if the result is nonsense instead of English. The fact that the result is nonsense is part of the proof that the word is not a verb. Imitate the examples.

Examples: carrier do carrier talking do talking
lasting do lasting management do management

1. employee ______________
2. pursue ______________
3. wastage ______________
4. willing ______________
5. preventable ______________
6. likely ______________
7. rescuing ______________
8. arrival ______________
9. approach ______________
10. receiver ______________
11. graduate ______________
12. connective ______________
13. lasting ______________
14. concentration ______________
15. momentary ______________
16. hastily ______________
17. being ______________
18. splash ______________
19. competitor ______________
20. doing ______________

Practice U: ADDING THE *DO* SUBSTITUTION INSIDE SENTENCES JUST FOR WORDS OTHER THAN THOSE THAT END IN S/ES OR ED AND OTHER THAN IRREGULAR VERBS IN THEIR PAST TENSE

[From text, page 121]

DIRECTIONS: For all the words (except the first) in these sentences, USE THE ***DO*** SUBSTITUTE SPELLING. DO THIS **IN YOUR HEAD**. Write out the TWO WORDS of the substitution **ONLY if the word that you are testing can be a verb both apart from the sentence and in the context of the whole sentence.** Imitate the example.

Example: The tiny strawberries that ^ [**do grow**] grow near here ^ [**do feed**] feed the animals mostly.

1. Ants scurry about doing the work that they prefer.
2. Many dislike studying with music on because of the distraction.
3. When deer stand in the road at night they fix their gaze on the lights of an on-coming car.
4. Trees that bend in a breeze rebound in time for the next gust.

Practice V: Adding the *Does*, *Did* or *Do* Substitutions for All Words

[From text, page 121]

Directions: For all the words (except the first) in these sentences, WRITE OUT THE *DOES, DO,* OR *DID* SUBSTITUTE SPELLING. DO THIS **IN YOUR HEAD**. Write out the TWO WORDS of the substitution **ONLY if the word that you are testing can be a verb both apart from the sentence and in the context of the whole sentence**. Imitate the example.

Example: I ^ [do think] think that the ticket my brother ^ [did get] got for speeding ^ [does make] makes him drive slower.

1. The busy office worker found that his overweight condition prevented him from playing the kind of tennis he once prided himself on.

2. When a youth finds a job that he likes and that pays well, he exerts all his energy to keep it.

3. When Sherry brought her broken earring to be repaired, the cost made her regret her carelessness.

4. The splattered bacon grease stung and made me use more caution.

5. The delayed decision gave enough time for gathering added information.

6. After Rose lost one earring , she threw the other away.

7. The forecast announced on last night's newscast proved to be incorrect.

8. Though hay contains nutritional value for cows, it contains none for us.

Practice W: Adding the *Does, Did,* or *Do* Substitutions after Carrying out the Helpers plus What/Ing Word Verb Test

[From text, page 121]

Directions: For each of these sentences, use **both** the Helpers plus What/Ing Word Verb Test **and** the Do/Does/Did Test (to find and label all verbs). Imitate the example.

Example: When you ^ [do leave] leave fruit trees untended, they can develop diseases that could kill them.

Important Note: From now on, you may do all testing for the Do/does/did Test in your head. **You must write out the two words** of the substitution **only when the word that you are testing can be a verb both apart from the sentence and in the context of the whole sentence**.

1. Since the arrival of word processors, personal letters from advertisers have flooded the mail; but an alert reader knows that such personalized mail is the result of mass advertising.

2. The experienced guide led the sightseers through the cave that had formed ages earlier and that now was filled with impressive stalagmites and stalactites.

3. When a drought begins to last for months, people who ordinarily don't think about how much water they are using will begin to use it cautiously.

4. When his younger brother slid into third base, he twisted his ankle so badly that he was grounded for the rest of the season.

5. The papers scattered across the fairground were so numerous that one could lose hope of ever seeing it clean again.

6. The star that is nearest to our sun stands trillions of miles distant from it.

Practice X: CARRYING OUT BOTH VERB TESTS

[From text, page 122]

DIRECTIONS: For each of these sentences, **CARRY OUT THE STEPS TO FOLLOW TO SUCCEED**—both the HELPERS PLUS WHAT/ING WORD VERB TEST and DO/DOES/DID VERB TEST.

1. When I drove to the bank and found it had closed because of a holiday, I knew that I should have paid more attention to the paper.
2. When an ad says that you will save money if you buy a certain product, it is not saying that you will save money if you did not intend to buy that product in the first place.
3. A fellow who fails to look in the mirror before he heads for work may find that his collar is turned up or that his sport coat has not been buttoned properly.
4. Chances taken behind the wheel of a car have sometimes caused severe accidents that could have been easily prevented if patience and willingness to arrive at one's destination slightly later had won out.
5. When one considers the beauty, variety, and great number of living things on earth , his or her thoughts must turn to the Higher Power that has given them to us.
6. When the vacuum cleaner recently quit working, a phone call to a salesman caused him to bring to the house both an outdated model and a rebuilt one, both of which could be afforded by the homeowner.

Practice Y: CARRYING OUT BOTH VERB TESTS

[From text, page 122]

DIRECTIONS: For each of these sentences, **CARRY OUT THE STEPS TO FOLLOW TO SUCCEED**—both the HELPERS PLUS WHAT/ING WORD VERB TEST and the DO/DOES/DID VERB TEST.

There was a time when a student who smoked was thought to be "cool." This is no longer true in many places. I know students who have a hatred for smoking, if not for smokers. They complain of the gagging pollution of the air, the stench on the smoker's breath, and the reek and filth of the ashtrays left with butts in them. Their disgust is not caused by the fact that smokers pollute their own bodies so much as by the fact that they sabotage the quality of living for others. They cheer whenever a law prohibits smoking in some new place. In fact, they seek the abolishment of the cigarette itself.

* * * * *

PARAGRAPH AND ESSAY SUPPLEMENT

LISTING AND SIGNPOSTS

GOALS IN THIS MINI-CHAPTER

To practice using a strategy for finding ANGLES by means of which you can discover more and better things to say about a topic—and to practice writing paragraphs by a listing of supporting details.

Chief Categories as "Angles"

There are a dozen or so especially helpful CATEGORIES or "angles" by means of which you can find new ways to look at a topic. A different angle or category often suggests fresh things to write about. Use these categories as a help for developing interesting and worthwhile essays.

The chief categories or "angles" are:

ADVANTAGES	*MISCONCEPTIONS*	*EXAMPLES*
DISADVANTAGES	*LIKENESSES*	*REMEDIES*
TIPS	*DIFFERENCES*	*REASONS*
OBJECTIONS	*STEPS*	*PROOF*
CAUSES	*PRECAUTIONS*	*REQUIREMENTS*

Paragraph by Listing

A paragraph by listing is a paragraph in which the topic idea—which is stated in a topic sentence—is supported by a LISTING OF SUPPORTING EVIDENCE OR DETAILS. Most paragraphs that develop a topic sentence are of this type.

Signposts to Help the Reader

The purpose of most paragraphs is to develop a topic idea (as expressed in a topic sentence). These paragraphs usually require a listing of details in support of their topic idea. GOOD WRITERS USE SIGNPOSTS TO TELL THEIR READERS WHEN THEY ARE ADDING ANOTHER DETAIL.

Use this list of common signposts—WITH AS MUCH VARIETY AS POSSIBLE—in all your writing:

ANOTHER	*NEXT*	*FIRST*
IN ADDITION	*ONE MORE*	*SECOND(LY), ETC.*
MOREOVER	*FINAL(LY)*	*TO START WITH*
BESIDES . . .	*ALSO*	*LAST(LY)*

Practice AA: Planning a Paragraph with Tips

Directions: Think of some TIPS that you could write in connection with any subtopic in one of these general subject areas: gardening, cooking, playing a particular game or sport, driving, biking, swimming, exercising, studying, and so forth. Write out FIVE statements that you might be able to write enough about to fill a paragraph. These statements will be possible TOPIC SENTENCES. Imitate the examples supplied below.

Examples

Here are some tips for remembering better.
If you want to make French toast, these tips should help you.
A gardener has these tips for helping transplants do well.

Practice BB: Outlining a Paragraph with Tips

Directions: Choose two of your statements from Practice AA, and add from THREE to FIVE OR MORE items after each—in outline form—to support your statement. Imitate the example outline supplied below.

Example Outline

Here are some tips for remembering better:
Getting enough sleep
Writing out the content first
Using my own words
Testing myself
Repeating—without looking—often

Practice CC: Writing a Paragraph with Tips

Directions: Choose one of your outlines from Practice BB, and develop a paragraph—whose first sentence is your topic sentence—based on it. Be sure to use as many signposts as possible. Imitate the example paragraph supplied below.

Example Paragraph

Here are some tips that I have discovered for remembering better. *First, I always remember better when I have gotten enough sleep. Next, I like to write out what I need to remember. I rewrite it in my own words when I can. The third help is to cover what I have written and test whether I can remember all of it—until I can. Finally, I must keep testing my memory in this way when the content being remembered is important enough.*

Practice DD: PLANNING A PARAGRAPH WITH ADVANTAGES OR REQUIREMENTS

DIRECTIONS: Follow the directions of Practice AA but use the aspect ADVANTAGES or REQUIREMENTS instead of tips. Imitate the examples supplied below.

Examples

THERE ARE MANY ADVANTAGES TO PLANTING TOMATOES.
A BIKE WITH A HEADLIGHT HAS IMPORTANT ADVANTAGES.
THERE ARE ADVANTAGES TO STUDYING WITH ENOUGH LIGHT.
THERE ARE SEVERAL REQUIREMENTS TO BE A GOOD LISTENER.
HERE ARE SOME REQUIREMENTS TO BE A GOOD COOK.

Practice EE: OUTLINING A PARAGRAPH WITH ADVANTAGES OR REQUIREMENTS

DIRECTIONS: Choose two of your statements from Practice DD, and add from THREE to FIVE OR MORE items after each—in outline form—to support your statement. Imitate the example outline supplied below.

Example Outline

THERE ARE MANY ADVANTAGES TO PLANTING TOMATOES:
Tomatoes to eat off the vine
Tomatoes for salads
Tomatoes for canning
More tomatoes to eat because cheaper
Tomatoes for frying
Tomatoes in the fall

Practice FF: WRITING A PARAGRAPH WITH ADVANTAGES OR REQUIREMENTS

DIRECTIONS: Choose one of your outlines from Practice EE, and develop a paragraph—whose first sentence is your topic sentence—based on it. Be sure to use as many signposts as possible. Imitate the example paragraph supplied below.

Example Paragraph

THOSE WHO GROW THEIR OWN TOMATOES REAP MANY ADVANTAGES. First, they can pluck a tomato off the vine and eat it right there whenever they wish. In addition, there is an abundance of tomatoes available for salads and cooking. Moreover, some may want to can home-grown tomatoes for use in later months. Lastly, tomatoes can be stored green in a basement and eaten after the growing season is over as they ripen naturally.

Chapter 8

Simpler Questions

Practice A: Taking Note of End Punctuation

[From text, page 138]

Directions: For each of these sentences, **UNDERLINE THE QUESTION MARK AT THE END OF THE SENTENCE**. (The purpose here is simply to give you practice in paying attention to the punctuation at the end of the sentence.) Imitate the example.

Example: Does the temperature drop significantly on rainy days?

1. Couldn't the deer that live in the nearby fields destroy young fruit trees?
2. Shouldn't the answers that are trickiest be supplied by the author?
3. Do vendors in the West sell Dr. Pepper?
4. Can't redwood trees grow wider than some buildings?
5. Wouldn't the librarian who is on duty be the one to ask for such information?
6. Isn't a twister a storm that can swallow a house?
7. Shouldn't a tree whose branches are dying be cut down?
8. Haven't flat hilltops served as landing fields in emergencies?
9. Don't people tire of spending their time watching TV?
10. Isn't the redness of the leaves at the tip of maple trees in spring a sign of new growth?

Practice B: Labeling the Movable Starter in Starter-Verb Questions

[From text, page 138]

Directions: For each of the sentences in Practice A, **LABEL THE STARTER AT THE BEGINNING OF THE QUESTION** (for now, this will also be at the beginning of the sentence). Imitate the example.

MS
Example: Does the temperature drop significantly on rainy days?

Practice C: Repositioning the Movable Starter in Starter-Verb Questions

[From text, page 139]

Directions: For each of the sentences in Practice A, **REPOSITION THE STARTER TO THE PLACE INSIDE THE SENTENCE WHERE IT BEST FITS. Use a caret (^) to show the place of insertion**, and **add side brackets to show that it is an editor's change**. Imitate the example.

MS [does]
Example: Does the temperature ^ drop significantly on rainy days?

Note: You do **not** need to change the question mark to a period, though you may do so if you wish.

Practice D: Labeling Main subjects in Starter-Verb Questions

[From text, page 139]

Directions: For each of the sentences in Practice A, **LABEL AS SUBJECT THE WORDS BETWEEN THE TWO POSITIONS OF THE MOVABLE STARTER THAT BELONG TOGETHER AS SUBJECT**. Imitate the example.

MS Ⓢ [does]
Example: Does the temperature ^ drop significantly on rainy days?

Practice E: CARRYING OUT STEPS 1–4

[From text, page 139]

DIRECTIONS: For these sentences, **CARRY OUT THE MAIN SUBJECT TEST—FOR QUESTIONS, STEPS 1 THROUGH 4**. Imitate the example.

MS ⓢ [should]

Example: Should a student who leaves his work home ^ be penalized?

1. Can one day of springtime rain cause severe flooding?
2. Couldn't driving for miles on a flat tire be harmful?
3. Shouldn't the hidden costs be listed by an honest seller?
4. Could birds that have built nests near the ground lose them because of flooding?
5. Can cars whose engines haven't been adjusted run on substitute fuels?
6. Isn't a sunset that is breath-taking one of the marvels of the world?
7. Don't all caterpillars turn into butterflies?
8. Shouldn't newspapers that are over a week old be discarded?
9. Wouldn't your younger brother ask for permission?
10. Couldn't a file cabinet that is overflowing be weeded of its junk?

Practice F: LABELING COMPANION VERBS TO THE MOVABLE STARTER IN STARTER-VERB QUESTIONS

[From text, page 140]

DIRECTIONS: For the sentences in Practice E, **CARRY OUT STEP 5**—that is, **locating and labeling companion verbs (if any) that follow the movable starter in its INSIDE POSITION**. Imitate the example.

MS ⓢ [should]

Example: Should a student who leaves his work home ^ be penalized?

Practice G: CARRYING OUT THE MAIN SUBJECT TEST—FOR QUESTIONS

[From text, page 141]

DIRECTIONS: For all of these sentences, **CARRY OUT THE ENTIRE MAIN SUBJECT TEST—FOR QUESTIONS**. Imitate the example.

Example: MS Didn't [(S) the person who planned this building] [didn't] ^ realize that too much lighting is wasteful?

1. Aren't the radio waves that have recently been discovered in space the effect of the explosion that caused our universe?
2. Wouldn't two days by the ocean be more than enough if it rained all the time?
3. Can't the webbing for a lawn chair that has become worn be replaced by something that is relatively inexpensive?
4. Couldn't a boat's speed ever beat the speed that a car can go at?
5. Don't the needles of a larch tree fall to the ground after they change their color just like leaves fall?
6. Isn't a book more interesting if we already know something about its subject?
7. Did the excuse that was given sound as if it had been concocted?
8. Can't it be said that success results from hard work?
9. Is the reason why you are leaving that you have another appointment?
10. Could the solutions be being found by a computer that is superfast?

Practice H: CARRYING OUT TESTS 2 AND 3

[From text, page 141]

DIRECTIONS: For the sentences in Practice G, **CARRY OUT TESTS 2 AND 3**—namely, the Helpers plus WHAT/ING Word Verb Test and the Do/does/did Test. Imitate the example.

Example: MS Didn't [(S) the person who ^ [did plan] planned this building] [didn't] ^ realize that too much lighting is wasteful?

Practice J: CARRYING OUT TESTS 1, 2 AND 3

[From text, page 141]

DIRECTIONS: For these sentences, carry out all three tests—namely, the Main Subject Test—for Questions, the Helpers plus WHAT/ING Word Verb Test, and the Do/does/did Test.

1. Shouldn't a lawn mower with a broken muffler be considered something that is unsafe for use?
2. Doesn't the smog that forms in cities cause many lung problems for those who must inhale it?
3. Shouldn't the air conditioners in buses be used only if the temperature inside the bus requires it?
4. Doesn't the loudness of the music in earphones cause deafness if the listener turns the volume too high?
5. Don't people who live near brooks see a greater variety of birds that are unusual?
6. Aren't those who live upright lives both happier and more successful at whatever they do?
7. Wouldn't a raccoon that has rabies bite a person who comes too close?
8. Doesn't a full breakfast give students the energy that they need throughout the morning?

Practice K: CARRYING OUT ALL TESTS

[From text, page 141]

DIRECTIONS: For these sentences, **CARRY OUT ALL THREE TESTS (AND THEIR STEPS) IN CORRECT ORDER.**

1. Doesn't a person who graduates from college earn a much higher salary than someone who has finished only high school?
2. Wouldn't a carpenter who takes pride in his work be someone whom you would recommend to everyone?
3. Have the skateboards that are more expensive become less of a cause of crippling injuries?
4. Aren't the memories that we have of when we were young the memories that make the deepest impression?
5. Isn't a person who can fix sickly computers like a doctor who cures a sickly person?
6. Aren't answers that come close to being right better than those that are not even near?
7. Might a student who has taken charge of his own learning regret the many benefits that result from this?
8. Shouldn't parents of a large family buy groceries when they are on sale and in large quantities?

PARAGRAPH AND ESSAY SUPPLEMENT

COHERENCE

GOAL IN THIS MINI-CHAPTER

To practice the strategies that "glue together" or INTERCONNECT sentences and paragraphs—that is, the strategies that cause COHERENCE.

REPETITION, CONSISTENCY, AND ECHOING AS "GLUE"

Readers need reminders and consistency. They want writers to interconnect what they say in these ways especially: (1) REPEAT the subject matter of paragraphs and essays (use the same wording or similar wording); (2) BE CONSISTENT in your use of pronouns and tenses; (3) use ECHOING—that is, remind readers of your viewpoint with respect to your topic from time to time (as the occasion arises).

Below is a list of strategies for keeping your writing INTERCONNECTED and CONSISTENT (with examples in bold and capitalized lettering). Put these strategies to constant use.

REPETITION OF TOPIC:	*The benefits of writing clearly ...* ***WRITING CLEARLY CAUSES . . .***
REPETITION OF CATEGORIZING WORD:	*Benefits ...* ***BENEFITS***
USE OF **SYNONYMS**:	*Benefits ...* ***ADVANTAGES***
USE OF **PARAPHRASING**:	*Benefits ...* ***HELPFUL EFFECTS***
USE OF **PRONOUNS**:	*Benefits ...* ***THEY***
USE OF **COGNATES** [FROM SAME ROOT]:	*Benefits ...* ***BENEFITING***
CONSISTENCY IN PRONOUN REFERENCE:	*Benefits ...* ***THEY ... THEM ... THEIR ... THEY***
CONSISTENCY IN TENSE:	*Benefited ...* ***HELPED***
PARALLEL STRUCTURE [USE OF THE SAME GRAMMATICAL STRUCTURE IN PAIRS AND SERIES]	*Benefited the writer* AND ***HELPED THE READER***

Practice L: PLANNING A PARAGRAPH LISTING DISADVANTAGES OR EXAMPLES

DIRECTIONS: Pick a topic that you feel strongly about—such as the disadvantages or the boredom CONNECTED WITH camping, long car rides, sewing, cooking, doing chores, and so forth. Then state the "point to be discussed" in an expression such as "There are disadvantages to . . ." or "There are many examples of . . ." Next list the points you will make to develop or prove your position—in outline form. Imitate the example outline supplied below.

Example Outline

THERE ARE DISADVANTAGES TO COOKING IN SOMEONE ELSE'S KITCHEN

Items that must be located:

- *Fry pan*
- *Margarine*
- *Kitchen knife*

Problems:

- *Finding right size fry pan*
- *Figuring how fast food will cook in this type fry pan*

Using a different kind of burner control

Practice M: WRITING A PARAGRAPH LISTING DISADVANTAGES OR EXAMPLES

DIRECTIONS: Write a paragraph based on the outline you prepared for Practice L. Make sure that you use as much repetition and echoing as the subject matter requires. Also be consistent in your use of pronoun reference and tenses. Imitate the example paragraph supplied below (note the THREE versions of the same paragraph, each of which has a different strand of "repetition" highlighted).

Example Paragraph—with Highlighting of Words That Say, Repeat, or Echo the Viewpoint "Disadvantage"

THERE ARE DISADVANTAGES TO TRYING TO COOK IN SOMEONE ELSE'S KITCHEN. *The first* ***disadvantage*** *is that you must locate exactly where the other person keeps specific cooking supplies—for example, the fry pan, the cooking utensils, and the pot holders. Another* ***disadvantage*** *is that you must decide whether the other person even has margarine and, if so, in what kind of container. One more* ***drawback*** *is that you must stand watch over the food for fear that this person's type of cookware cooks faster than the cookware that you are used to. The whole experience is filled with* ***uncertainty*** *and* ***unhappiness.***

Example Paragraph—with Highlighting of Words That Say, Repeat, or Echo the Wording "Someone Else"

THERE ARE DISADVANTAGES TO TRYING TO COOK IN SOMEONE ELSE'S KITCHEN. The first disadvantage is that you must locate exactly where the ***other person*** *keeps specific cooking supplies—for example, the fry pan, the cooking utensils, and the pot holders. Another disadvantage is that you must decide whether the* ***other person*** *even has margarine and, if so, in what kind of container. One more drawback is that you must stand watch over the food for fear that* ***this person****'s type of cookware cooks faster than the cookware that you are used to. The whole experience is filled with uncertainty and unhappiness.*

Example Paragraph—with Highlighting of Words That Say, Repeat, or Echo the Word "Cook"

THERE ARE DISADVANTAGES TO TRYING TO COOK IN SOMEONE ELSE'S KITCHEN. The first disadvantage is that you must locate exactly where the other person keeps specific ***cooking supplies—for example, the fry pan, the cooking utensils, and the pot holders****. Another disadvantage is that you must decide whether the other person even has* ***margarine and, if so, in what kind of container****. One more drawback is that you must stand* ***watch over the food*** *for fear that this person's* ***type of cookware cooks faster*** *than the* ***cookware that you are used to****. The whole experience is filled with uncertainty and unhappiness.*

[Notice that the wording ***the whole experience*** is an echoing of ***trying to cook in someone else's kitchen*—and of all the details that gave examples of the problems involved**. There are also two examples of parallel structure: the series of noun clusters ***the fry pan, the cooking utensils,*** and ***the pot holders***; and the two nouns that are the objects of the preposition *with*—namely: ***uncertainty*** and ***unhappiness***. Finally, one more type of consistency was the repeated use of the pronoun *you*; the writer did **not** switch to *I* or to *one (a person).*]

MISCONCEPTION

A MISCONCEPTION is a misunderstanding that someone has about the truth of some matter. For example, it is a misconception to believe that insufficient sleep causes no harm to a person.

PRACTICE N: PLANNING A PARAGRAPH LISTING REASONS OR MISCONCEPTIONS

DIRECTIONS: Plan to write a paragraph about either REASONS for some truth or about MISCONCEPTIONS people have about something you feel strongly about—such as computers, studying, newspapers, magazines (a magazine), programs (a program) on TV, city/country living, and so forth. Be sure to write about a narrower point than just, say, "*studying*"—for example, you could write about "*MISCONCEPTIONS PEOPLE HAVE ABOUT WHAT CAUSES SUCCESSFUL LEARNING.*" Then state the "point to be discussed" in an expression such as "There are reasons why . . ." or "It is a misconception some people have that . . ." Next list the points you will make to develop or prove your position—in outline form. Imitate the example outline supplied below.

Example Outline

IT IS A MISCONCEPTION THAT OVERTIREDNESS HAS NO EFFECT ON LEARNING

Fall asleep in class
Fall asleep at study
Cut study short
Can't remember on quizzes and tests
Can't keep up with note-taking
Can't learn well enough to remember the next day

Practice P: WRITING A PARAGRAPH LISTING REASONS OR MISCONCEPTIONS

DIRECTIONS: Write a paragraph based on the outline you prepared for Practice N. Make sure that you use as much repetition and echoing as the subject matter requires. Also be consistent in your use of pronoun reference and tenses. Be sure to also use signposts when they are appropriate. Imitate the example paragraph supplied below.

Example Paragraph

IT IS A MISCONCEPTION FOR STUDENTS TO BELIEVE THAT OVERTIREDNESS HAS LITTLE INFLUENCE ON THEIR ABILITY TO DO WELL IN SCHOOL. *The most serious result of students' fatigue is its interference with their ability to keep up with their teachers in class—either in note-taking or in registering mentally all that they say. Another effect is their resultant inability to absorb material when studying outside of class. The tendency for such students in both situations—if it is not to fall asleep—is to plod along without gain and ignore their pokiness of mind. One more harmful effect of student fatigue is the resultant incapacity to understand questions on tests and quizzes fast enough and then to extract the answers from their memory quickly enough to even get a passing grade, not to mention score their best. Finally, and the greatest shame of all, is that such students think the world is proceeding at their pace when the truth is that they are proceeding at a snail's pace.*

Chapter 9

The Helper That Shifts—in Statements

Practice A: Carrying out Tests 2–4

[From text, page 152]

Directions: For these sentences, **first** carry out both the Helpers plus What/Ing Word Verb Test and the Do/does/did Test. **Second**, reposition the starter and test the question for grammatical fit. **Third,** label the starter—in its inside position—with the lettering **MS**. Imitate the example.

Example: [does] ^ The beauty of a sunset ^ [~~does~~ depend] (MS) ~~depends~~ on many factors.

Note: You do **not** need to change the period to a question mark, though you may do so if you wish.

1. The Sunday newspaper takes longer to read.
2. Students attending Sunday school should get only lively instruction.
3. Gutters with leaves cause homeowners headaches.
4. Franklin Delano Roosevelt was the President for his times.
5. Some small birds remain north until the first frost.
6. Circling hawks can screech at certain times of the year.
7. File folders with five tab settings are handier than those with only three.
8. Handwritten lists surpass computer-stored ones in simplicity and availability.

Practice B: FINDING AND LABELING MOVABLE STARTERS WITH *N'T* ATTACHED

[From text, page 155]

DIRECTIONS: For these sentences, **first** CARRY OUT BOTH THE HELPERS PLUS WHAT/ING WORD VERB TEST AND THE DO/DOES/DID TEST. **Second**, REPOSITION THE STARTER—WITH *N'T* ATTACHED—AT THE START OF THE STATEMENT. **Third,** LABEL IT AS THE MOVABLE STARTER. Imitate the example.

Example: [isn't] ^ A cat ~~isn't~~ (MS) mindful of passing cars.

1. Answers aren't always provided in texts.

2. Some wildflowers aren't destroyed by frost.

3. Her effort wasn't sufficient to earn an "A."

4. The dog wasn't barking because of vengefulness.

5. The drivers in the parkway weren't expecting the delay.

6. The TV reception couldn't be improved.

7. The days didn't seem to be long enough.

8. Blue jays aren't as common in late spring and summer.

Practice C: FINDING AND LABELING MOVABLE STARTERS FOLLOWED BY *NOT*

[From text, page 156]

DIRECTIONS: For these sentences, **first** FORM ANY CONTRACTIONS FOR *NOT* WITH THE STARTER BEFORE IT. **Second**, CARRY OUT THE HELPERS PLUS WHAT/ING WORD VERB TEST AND THE DO/DOES/DID TEST. **Finally**, REPOSITION THE MOVABLE STARTER AT THE FRONT OF THE STATEMENT AND LABEL IT AS THE MOVABLE STARTER. Imitate the example.

Example: [weren't] ^ The sentences ^ MS [~~weren't~~] ~~were not~~ clear.

1. A delay of one minute does not always seem short.

2. A child of three does not like to be left behind.

3. Rooms without sufficient light are not suitable for study.

4. A new car is not always an unused car.

5. Unplowed meadows do not remain meadows long.

6. A quick review will not always be the right approach.

7. An extension cord is not always a safe solution.

8. Fluorescent lighting has not replaced the light bulb.

Practice D: More Finding and Labeling of Movable Starters Followed by *Not*

[From text, page 156]

Directions: For these sentences, carry out the same directions as for Practice C.

1. Cold days do not seem as cold if the wind is not blowing.
2. Scattered clouds do not provide shade while heavy clouds do not let the sun's rays through.
3. A bird is not as welcome when it does not have neighborly habits.
4. An answer is not acceptable when the student does not write his/her neatest.
5. Wild animals cannot be blamed if they do not fear the danger of a speeding car.
6. Summers cannot be as enjoyable when a student is not free of school work.

Practice E: Finding and Labeling of Movable Starters

[From text, page 156]

Directions: For these sentences, follow the directions for Practice C.

1. Students do not do well on tests when they have not read the questions carefully.
2. Nothing lasts very long if you do not care for it.
3. Studying is its own reward when a student gives it his/her all.
4. Branches should not touch electric wires if this can be avoided.
5. Orchards must be sprayed if the owner does not wish inferior fruit.
6. Decayed limbs are hazardous to lumberjacks who are cutting down trees.

Practice F: Writing out the *Do/does/did* Substitutions for *Do, Does,* and *Did*

[From text, page 158]

Directions: In the space beside each word, WRITE OUT ITS DO/DOES/DID SUBSTITUTE SPELLING. Use **two words**.

DID = ______________ *DOES* = ______________ *DID* = --------------

Practice G: Carrying out the *Do/Does/Did* Substitutions for *Do, Does, and Did* when Main Verbs

[From text, page 158]

Directions: For these sentences, MAKE THE CORRECT *DO/DOES/DID* SUBSTITUTION. Imitate the example.

[does do]
Example: Jean ^ does her assignments carefully.

1. Sensible students do their best work on every assignment.
2. An unbraked car does better than 50 m.p.h. on steep hills.
3. Some students do their least interesting assignments first.
4. No one did anything about the pothole.
5. A teenager does less than an adult's share often.
6. All did their best.
7. Computers do their work with precision.
8. Everyone does his/her job.

Practice H: Writing out the *Do/does/did* Substitutions for *Have, Has,* and *Had*

[From text, page 158]

Directions: In the space beside each word, WRITE OUT ITS DO/DOES/DID SUBSTITUTE SPELLING. Use TWO WORDS.

HAVE = ____________

HAS = ____________

HAD = ____________

Practice J: CARRYING OUT THE *DO/DOES/DID* SUBSTITUTIONS FOR *HAVE, HAS, AND HAD* WHEN MAIN VERBS

[From text, page 159]

DIRECTIONS: For these sentences, MAKE THE CORRECT *DO / DOES / DID* SUBSTITUTION. Imitate the example.

[did have]
Example: We ^ had no time to rest.

1. Those of voting age have the privilege of choosing their representatives in government.
2. No one had any interest in the suggestion.
3. Roofs often have frost on them on clear winter mornings.
4. No one has a monopoly on intelligent ideas.
5. Extra thick windows have either two or three panes of glass.
6. A gnarled tree has a beauty of its own.
7. Everyone has at least one question about grammar.
8. Most had a thoroughly enjoyable time.

Practice K: CARRYING OUT THE *DO/DOES/DID* SUBSTITUTIONS FOR *DO, DOES, DID, HAVE, HAS,* AND *HAD* WHEN MAIN VERBS

[From text, page 159]

DIRECTIONS: For these sentences, MAKE THE CORRECT *DO / DOES / DID* SUBSTITUTION.

1. Many have problems with cracks in their sidewalks.
2. Some do less than enough of their work.
3. No one had all the headaches.
4. Some carpenters do everything but roofs.
5. Each has a different task.
6. No one does everything.
7. The principal has a solution.
8. Marsha did the best of all.

Practice L: CARRYING OUT TESTS 2–4 AND COVERING INSIDE STARTERS

[From text, page 160]

DIRECTIONS: For these sentences, CARRY OUT TESTS 2–4—the Helpers plus WHAT/ING Word Verb Test, the Do/does/did Test, and the Movable Starter Test. Be sure to cover the inside starter as you test. Imitate the example.

Example: [does] ^ The whiteness of snow ^ [MS: ~~does~~ brighten] ~~brightens~~ scenery.

1. Masonite paneling sometimes looks like wood.

2. A chipped dish might still have lots of life.

3. We do all our work.

4. Some families say a prayer before meals.

5. Cooler indoor temperatures could be the cause of greater healthfulness.

6. We expected no surprises.

7. Broken glass has jagged edges.

8. One poor quiz mark wasn't enough of a shock for Tim.

9. Computers are not that difficult to use.

10. Piles of unfinished work cluttered the floor.

Practice M: More Carrying out of Tests 2–4 and Covering of Inside Starters

[From text, page 160]

Directions: For these sentences, carry out the directions for Practice L. **You must test each verb**. Imitate the example.

Example: [will] ^ A mist that <u>can be seen</u> at dawn MS ~~will~~ <u>vanish</u> with the arrival of the sun.

1. A watch that might lose speed is less helpful than one that might gain speed.

2. A lamp that has lasted thirty years has served its owner well.

3. Typewriters have joined the ranks of machines that are outdated.

4. Video cameras are becoming as common as movie cameras once were.

5. Leaves that can twirl in the wind can hang motionless on a still day.

6. The berries that the birds do not eat are available for human consumption.

7. The day when the lake was emptied was a sorry one.

8. The use of an index can save time that is precious.

Practice N: CARRYING OUT TESTS 2–4 WHILE COVERING INSIDE STARTERS AND ORIGINAL STARTERS + *NOT*

[From text, page 161]

DIRECTIONS: For these sentences, CARRY OUT TESTS 2–4—namely, the Helpers plus WHAT/ING Word Verb Test, the Do/does/did Test, and the Movable Starter Test. **Be sure to cover both the inside starter and any original starter, as well as any accompanying *not* that you rewrote as a contraction**. Imitate the example.

MS

[doesn't] [~~doesn't~~]

Example: ^ A humming bird ^ ~~does not~~ visit very many flowers at a time.

1. Their unlisted number was not obtainable.

2. Some pets are not allowed indoors.

3. Weight lifting does not count as aerobic exercise.

4. Houses found on curves cannot be safe in slippery weather.

5. The view from this mountain is not especially memorable.

6. Joanne has not had time to reorganize her room.

Practice P: MORE CARRYING OUT OF TESTS 2–4 WHILE COVERING INSIDE STARTERS AND ORIGINAL STARTERS + *NOT*

[From text, page 161]

DIRECTIONS: For these sentences, CARRY OUT TESTS 2–4—namely, the Helpers plus WHAT/ING Word Verb Test, the Do/does/did Test, and the Movable Starter Test. **Be sure to cover both the inside starter and any original starter, as well as any accompanying *not* that you rewrote as a contraction**. THERE MAY BE EXTRA VERBS in these sentences, so you must test EACH of them. Imitate the example.

Example: [haven't] ^ The planes that have been flying overhead ^ [MS ~~[haven't]~~] ~~have not~~ intended to land.

1. The list that was made yesterday has not been forgotten yet.
2. Those who have not volunteered may be needed anyway.
3. The day has not yet come when there are no insects to be seen.
4. Packaging tapes that are dependable have not been hard to find.
5. A tree that has become diseased is not unappealing to woodpeckers.
6. The color of a meadow does not stay the same because the type of wildflowers can change.
7. A tree whose color has changed out of season is experiencing stress.
8. Telephone wires that have been buried are not free from damage from rodents.
9. A product that is not selling well should not be discarded until the company has tried different sorts of advertising.
10. Winter will not necessarily be milder because some days in November were unusually warm.

Practice Q: Carrying out Tests 2–4 while Covering Inside Starters and Original Main Verbs for a Substitute Spelling Now Being Tested

[From text, page 161]

Directions: For these sentences, CARRY OUT TESTS 2–4—namely, the Helpers plus WHAT/ING Word Verb Test, the Do/does/did Test, and the Movable Starter Test. **Be sure to cover all "extra" inside wording as you test**. Imitate the example.

MS
[does] **[~~does~~ tell]**
Example: ^ A dictionary ^ ~~tells~~ the origin of some words.

1. The desk's frail leg cracked because of the rough handling.

2. Acid rain poisons both fish and plants.

3. Easy chairs assist relaxation rather than concentration.

4. Many people with back trouble use exercises to prevent relapses.

5. A rain check allows a person to wait for a better sale.

6. Colorful birds choose hidden places to nest.

7. A catbird has a medley of songs.

8. Photocopying machines produce glossy copies.

Practice R: More Carrying out of Tests 2–4 while Covering Inside Starters and Original Main Verbs for a Substitute Spelling Now Being Tested

[From text, page 161]

Directions: For these sentences, carry out the Helpers plus WHAT/ING Word Verb Test, the Do/does/did Test, and the Movable Starter Test. These sentences have extra verbs **so you must test each of them**. Be sure to always cover the extra inside wording as you test. Imitate the example.

Example: [does] ^ An answer that is indistinct ^ [MS: [~~does~~ cause]] ~~causes~~ classmates to lose interest.

1. The clouds caused a coolness that was not expected.

2. The recipe that was tried lacked sufficient directions.

3. No one gave the answer that the teacher wanted.

4. The disks that were used in one computer failed to work in another.

5. A cat has less worries when the dog in the house is his friend.

6. A go-cart will not work if it lacks strong enough wheels.

7. Even weeds have flowers that are delicate.

8. Birds that are wary live longer.

Practice S: Carrying out Tests 2–4 while Using Only Original Wording for Verbs Not Now Being Tested

[From text, page 162]

Directions: For these sentences, CARRY OUT TESTS 2–4. **As you test for movable starters, be sure to use only the original wording for words not now being tested. Continue to cover all the extra inside wording as you test.** Imitate the example.

Example: [would] ^ The horse that [did like] ^ liked its freedom ~~would~~ MS repeatedly break the fence.

1. A youngster whose suggestions make sense should be heeded.

2. Waffles that stick to the waffle iron can be difficult to remove.

3. Drivers who have just gone through a puddle could find that their brakes have lost their gripping power.

4. A student returning home from college risks lives when he does not adjust his speed to weather conditions.

5. A homeowner who would add a picture window that will face south can not imagine how much warmer the sun can make the room in winter.

6. Books that are sitting in bookcases will be of benefit only to those who read them.

7. Groceries that are unusually heavy could break through an undoubled paper bag.

8. Few realized how serious the accident at the Three-Mile Island power plant was.

Practice T: USING A QUESTION-ASKING TONE OF VOICE AND PAUSING RIGHT WHEN ASKING SOMEONE ELSE'S QUESTION

[From text, page 163]

DIRECTIONS: SAY THESE QUESTIONS ALOUD. **Go out of your way to use a question-asking tone of voice, and pause clearly at the place of the dots**—the place where the movable starter would be if the question had been a statement.

1. Should a day in September ... be so cold that one has to wear a winter coat?

2. Would people who are always complaining about the weather ... be any better off if they lived on the other side of the equator?

3. Don't students who do their writing on a word processor ... find it much easier to make corrections?

4. Wouldn't you and all of your family ... say more to each other if the TV were turned off more?

5. Will Americans who love gas-guzzling cars ... someday learn how scarce oil can become?

6. Do people who are borrowers ... sometimes take the kindness of others too much for granted?

7. Can clothes that have gotten dyed by mistake ... be made white again easily?

8. Could a recipe that had not been tried before ... win disapproval before the first taste?

Practice U: CARRYING OUT TESTS 1–4 IN THEIR ENTIRETY

[From text, page 165]

DIRECTIONS: For these sentences, CARRY OUT TESTS 1–4 IN THEIR ENTIRETY. Imitate the example.

ms
[Isn't] [~~did become~~] [~~isn't~~]

Example: ^ The girl who ^ became president of our class ^ ~~is not~~ a member of the track team.

1. Shouldn't shoppers who want to take best advantage of sales arrive before items have been sold out?

2. The message for the teacher from an honest question is that this is a student who cares whether he or she is learning.

3. A temperature that hovers above freezing can not be the reason for precipitation in the form of snow.

4. Couldn't toddlers who awake before their family awakes have some breakfast left out for them so they won't waken others due to their hunger?

5. A farmer whose costs keep rising finds that his land does not pay his bills.

6. Don't children who grow up in a large family learn how they can get along with others at an early age?

Practice V: CARRYING OUT TESTS 1–4 IN THEIR ENTIRETY

[From text, page 165]

DIRECTIONS: For these sentences, CARRY OUT TESTS 1–4 IN THEIR ENTIRETY.

1. Can't a girl so overuse makeup that she repels boys rather than attracts them?

2. Few who have hunted deer in near-zero weather would not try it again provided that their hunting efforts proved successful.

3. Can't a deer be spotted more easily when a covering of snow makes his tan body more visible?

4. Will the liberal arts foundation that has served students well for centuries be abandoned now for subject matter that trains one for too narrow a career?

5. All students who have learned how they can use index cards to master a subject prefer this method over every other.

6. Where he can study the subjects that require concentration is the chief concern of a student whose house is noisy.

PARAGRAPH AND ESSAY SUPPLEMENT

ANECDOTE

GOAL IN THIS MINI-CHAPTER

To practice more with the paragraph developed by anecdote or story.

PARAGRAPH BY ANECDOTE

A paragraph developed by ANECDOTE is a paragraph that uses a story—that is, an incident that truly happened—to prove some point with respect to your topic. Besides holding the interest of your readers and whetting their appetites for more of the same, a paragraph of this sort is powerful as proof of some point or as a means to persuade readers to adopt a new attitude or to take a new course of action.

PRACTICE W: PLANNING A PARAGRAPH DEVELOPED BY AN ANECDOTE

DIRECTIONS: Think of a story in your own experience or the experience of a friend, acquaintance, or family member that you can use to draw a lesson from. Often an accident, mishap, or disaster of any sort suggests a lesson (or moral) that you would want to bring home to your reader. First state the lesson that the story teaches, the "point under discussion." Then list the details of the story that you will choose from as you write. Imitate the example outline supplied below.

Example Outline

DRIVING IN SNOWY CONDITIONS CAN CAUSE ACCIDENTS
Family in car
Subcompact
Intermittent heavy snow
No plows
Unable to stop at curve
Loss of two cars

Practice X: WRITING A PARAGRAPH DEVELOPED BY AN ANECDOTE

DIRECTIONS: Write a paragraph based on the outline you prepared for Practice W. Be sure to select all and only those details that will most vividly and effectively drive home the moral or lesson you are speaking to. Be sure to use repetition, consistency, and echoing effectively. Imitate the example paragraph supplied below.

Example Paragraph

SOMETIMES THE BEST TIP FOR DRIVERS IS THAT THEY STAY AT HOME. *There is one family I know that would have greatly benefited from such advice. Without forethought one forbidding January day, the father had set out with his wife and two small children in their subcompact car. Now and again their car would veer on the icy roads. The sometimes blinding snow would come only in squalls so that no plows were in sight. Almost no one else was on the road. Then it happened. At a curve just short of town, the car skidded so severely that the father could neither stop nor turn. An approaching driver did not sense the danger. The cars collided head on. Only Divine Providence kept the vehicles' occupants from serious injury; the cars themselves were unsalvageable.*

Practice Y: PLANNING AND WRITING A SECOND PARAGRAPH DEVELOPED BY AN ANECDOTE

DIRECTIONS: Choose another story that you can use to teach a lesson or moral and develop it into a paragraph following the directions of Practices W and X.

Chapter 10

Main Subjects in Statements

Practice A: Carrying out Tests 1–5

[From text, page 169]

Directions: For each of these sentences, CARRY OUT TESTS 1–5. Imitate the example.

Example: [does] ^ ⓢ [A very early riser] ^ MS [does see] sees the stars at their most beautiful.

1. Families with one TV channel can't argue over which program to watch.

2. Skill at keyboarding has now become a necessity.

3. Kitchen timers benefit anyone who needs a reminder.

4. A devoted dog seeks nearness to his master.

5. The mist over a valley has an eerie appearance.

6. A hungry cat won't ignore the scraps you have left on your plate.

7. Geese flying south form the shape of a "V."

8. Overhead telephone wires have not been eliminated everywhere.

Practice B: CARRYING OUT TESTS 1–5

[From text, page 169]

Directions: For each of these sentences, follow the directions for Practice A.

1. A box that is sturdy should not be discarded.

2. Couldn't the spraying that kills insects reduce the bird population?

3. The post office sells a book that has ZIP codes.

4. A book that you like should be shared.

5. Can an ant carry something that is heavier than itself?

6. Trees that have shallow roots can be easily blown over.

7. Can't you lose what you have stored in a computer?

8. You can check your success if you have made a list of goals.

Practice C: Carrying out Tests 1–5

[From text, page 169]

Directions: For each of these sentences, follow the directions for Practice A.

1. Boxes that contain discarded junk can only clutter an attic that receives them.

2. Shouldn't a person who wants to be successful seek the highest possible grade in every course?

3. The frost that kills plants in the garden causes trees to change color.

4. Won't a cat that has set its heart on a chipmunk be the victor if it continues stalking it?

5. Beaches where the sand is like silt are filled with Frisbee players when the warmer weather arrives.

6. The trees that have the richest colors in the Northeast are the maple trees that also provide maple sugar.

Practice D: Carrying out Tests 1–5 and Making Sure that the Words in the Subject Territory Sound as if They Belong Together

[From text, page 170]

Directions: For these sentences, **CARRY OUT TESTS 1–5. Be sure to test whether the words in the subject territory—between the Movable Starter's two positions—sound as if they belong together.** Imitate the example.

Example: [does] ^ A good pianist (Ⓢ) rarely (ADVB) ^ practices (MS [does practice]) less than daily.

1. Evenings during daylight savings time always seem longer.

2. Those who have done their own work never need to cheat.

3. Mosquitoes occasionally do their biting after summer is over.

4. Our family rarely went camping just for a weekend.

5. People who usually buy when things are on sale can more easily buy when the next sale comes.

6. An answer that just pops into the mind often lacks enough thought to be fully accurate.

7. A heat pump, which captures the heat in water, seldom supplies all the heat needed by a larger building.

8. Drivers of heavy equipment always signal when they are backing up.

Practice E: Carrying out Tests 1–5 and Making Sure that the Words in the Subject Territory Sound as if They Belong Together

[From text, page 170]

Directions: For these sentences, carry out the directions for Practice D.

1. Reminders that one forgets to look at rarely help at all.

2. The lined paper that students use in their loose-leaf binders rarely goes on sale any more.

3. A boy whose mind is on a project sometimes forgets that he must also eat.

4. Wouldn't a swim some place be a remedy for heat that leaves one sticky?

5. A dog that follows children all day always catches a nap when he returns.

6. A person who has not seen a falling star rarely sits on a hillside on a starlit night.

7. Does a mouse that seeks the warmth of a house have a chance when a cat is on the prowl?

8. Children often forget that broken glass can cause severe cuts.

Practice F: DETERMINING THE MEANING OF THE VERB *BE* IN SPACE-FILLER *THERE* SENTENCES

[From text, page 173]

Directions: REWRITE EACH OF THESE SENTENCES. **Omit the word *there*. Replace it with the words after the verb that fit, and substitute for the verb *BE* the meaning supplied for you in parentheses. Be sure to use the correct tense for this substitute.** Imitate the example.

Example: There were enough parking places. (**be at hand**) ➡

Enough parking places were at hand.

1. There are many thunderstorms. (**take place**)

   ____

2. There was little time for thinking. (**be at hand**)

   ____

3. There is a shortage of gasoline. (**exist** or **be at hand**)

   ____

4. There is an easy solution to many problems. (**exist** or **be at hand**)

   ____

5. There will be another rehearsal. (**take place**)

   ____

6. There are several kinds of sparrows. (**exist**)

   ____

7. There is room for one more. (**exist** or **be at hand**)

   ____

8. There could have been too long a delay. (**take place**)

   ____

9. There are few who question the need for adequate sleep. (**exist** or **be at hand**)

   ____

10. There is room for doubt. (**exist**)

   ____

Practice G: CARRYING OUT TESTS 1–5 AND LABELING SPACE-FILLER *THERE* CORRECTLY

[From text, page 173]

Directions: For the sentences in Practice F, CARRY OUT ALL THE TESTS AND STEPS. Imitate the example.

[is] ~~S~~→ MS Ⓢ [shouldn't]

Example: ^There is no reason why an honest question should ^not be asked.

Practice H: CARRYING OUT OF TESTS 1–5 AND LABELING OF SPACE-FILLER *THERE* CORRECTLY

[From text, page 173]

Directions: For these sentences, CARRY OUT ALL TESTS AND STEPS. (Check for the subject in your head). Imitate the example.

[were] ~~S~~→ MS Ⓢ

Example: ^There were enough parking places.

1. There are too many deer that cross roads.
2. Children whose parents both work often have extra responsibilities.
3. There are too few first-rate movies.
4. There were several earthquakes that registered high on the Richter scale.
5. Isn't this canyon the one that you remember?
6. There was no place where a traveler could stay cheaply.
7. There is another hiding place that you did not think of.
8. Our memory sometimes stores things that we may think we have forgotten.
9. Have you ever been confused as to what day it was?
10. There are many students who work at improving how they study.

Practice J: IDENTIFYING THE TRUE SUBJECT IN SPACE-FILLER *THERE* SENTENCES

[From text, page 174]

Directions: REWRITE EACH OF THESE SENTENCES. **Omit the word *there*. Replace it with only those words after the verb that fit. Be sure to also choose the best meaning for the verb *BE***—choose ***EXIST, TAKE PLACE, BE AT HAND,*** or ***BE PRESENT***. IMITATE THE EXAMPLE.

Example: There will be no practice tomorrow. ➡

No practice will take place tomorrow.

1. There are only sand dunes in the desert.

 ____

2. There is little hope for success if someone does not study.

 ____

3. There should be more muffins in the kitchen.

 ____

4. There was a long line at the theater last night.

 ____

5. There could be more rain if the low-pressure system stays.

 ____

6. There were more mountains behind the ones we could see.

 ____

7. There couldn't have been more than a dozen of us there.

 ____

8. There may be more bad news before the good news comes.

 ____

9. There was clutter wherever one looked.

 ____

10. There are a few pens in the drawer of the table.

 ____

Practice K: CARRYING OUT TESTS 1–5 IN THEIR ENTIRETY

[From text, page 174]

Directions: For these sentences, CARRY OUT TESTS 1–5. Imitate the example.

[will] Ⓢ→ MS Ⓢ

Example: ^ There will be no practice tomorrow.

1. Weren't the kindergartners who burst from the building quickly engulfed by the string of buses that had been waiting for them?
2. A person readily understands how the hungry robin finds enough food to feed itself and its young when he watches one at work.
3. There must be different ways to study because all students do not achieve the same degree of success.
4. A clock that wouldn't keep running in the thin air of the Alps might work perfectly when its owner returned to sea level.
5. The coffee tin that comes with a plastic cover has many uses for the camper who needs to keep things separate and dry.
6. There must be a reason why computers get more powerful because there is a new announcement almost every month.
7. Whoever reads the newspaper regularly keeps abreast of those events that may be shaping the future of our planet.
8. The stationmaster could not say when the train would arrive because there had been a fire at one of the stations.

Practice L: CARRYING OUT TESTS 1–5 IN THEIR ENTIRETY

[From text, page 174]

Directions: For these sentences, **CARRY OUT TESTS 1–5**. Imitate the example in Practice K.

There are pastimes that have engrossed people for centuries and that still have merit today. There is the time-honored crossword puzzle that is the very reason why some people buy a newspaper at all. There is also knitting, a productive pastime that can even be practiced while one watches TV. There is also the game of bridge that four can play and that can absorb couples for hours on end. Another pastime that too many enjoy simply for the money that they hope to make is poker. Isn't pinochle another game that people still enjoy playing though it has been being played in one form or another since the seventeenth century?

Practice M: WRITING SENTENCES USING SPACE-FILLER *THERE*

[From text, page 175]

Directions: WRITE THREE SENTENCES OF YOUR OWN THAT START WITH SPACE-FILLER *THERE*—not with *there* that means "in that place" or "over there." Imitate the example.

Example: There are precautions to take when you are cooking.

____

____

____

PARAGRAPH AND ESSAY SUPPLEMENT

DESCRIPTION

GOAL IN THIS MINI-CHAPTER

To practice describing objects adequately.

PARAGRAPH BY DESCRIPTION

An effective paragraph by DESCRIPTION not only mentions the physical characteristics of an object but also compares these characteristics with something readers can more clearly visualize. These paragraphs can add concreteness to your writing.

PRACTICE N: PLANNING A PARAGRAPH DEVELOPED BY DESCRIPTION

DIRECTIONS: Choose something extremely simple to describe, such as a breadboard, a piece of paper, a napkin, an eraser, a paper clip, a staple, and so forth. In your outline, start with a statement that identifies what you will describe (and its importance if relevant). Then, as the first of the "details," add some statement that compares the object AS A WHOLE to something it is most similar to. Then list all the other characteristics of the object—proceeding in some logical order, such as from left to right or top to bottom—both telling the object's features **and** comparing these to something every reader will have first-hand and instant knowledge and understanding of. The features to include are the dimensions of the whole (and of the parts, if any); the weight; the color; the shape; the relative position of the parts; and the texture (what it looks/feels like). Imitate the example outline supplied below.

Example Outline

AN ORDINARY PIECE OF UNUSED CHALK

Overall, like very short dowel or a sawed-off piece of a cylindrical wooden spoon's handle
Length of finger (3")
Shape of pen (cylindrical)
Diameter that's thicker than a pen's (2/5 of an inch)
Color: antiseptic white (white of refined white sugar)
Weight of simple teaspoon (about an ounce)
Appearance of something solid and flat-ended—at both ends (like a package of life savers)
Feel (texture) of a piece of glossy paper

Practice P: WRITING A PARAGRAPH DEVELOPED BY DESCRIPTION

DIRECTIONS: Write a paragraph based on the outline you prepared for Practice N. Be consistent in your use of pronoun reference and tenses. As you point out the location of parts, lettering, or color, be sure to pinpoint the location in terms of relative distance (add a comparison if this would be helpful) and direction. Imitate the example paragraph supplied below.

Example Paragraph

THE PIECE OF CHALK THAT I AM HOLDING IS NORMAL IN SIZE AND TEXTURE. Except for the fact that it is white, it has the appearance of a sawed-off, three-inch section of either a 2/5" thick dowel or a handle of a cylindrical wooden kitchen spoon. It has the length, then, of one's longest finger approximately. It is cylindrical in shape as a pen is but is slightly thicker. It has the diameter, roughly, of one's little finger. It is antiseptic white in color, odorless, and as smooth to feel as a piece of composition paper. It must weigh about the same as a simple, common tea-spoon—about an ounce. It is solid, of course, and—because not yet used—flat at both ends. It is a marking device that can be put to many uses.

Practice Q: PLANNING AND WRITING AN ESSAY WITH JUST DESCRIPTION

DIRECTIONS: Choose an object to describe that is slightly more complex than those suggested in Practice N—such as a letter opener, a ruler, a sugar bowl or vase, a simple tool, a simple kitchen device, and so forth. Divide your task into groups of things (that belong together) that you will describe—for example, its various dimensions in one group, its coloring and appearance in another, and the rest of its features in still a third. In both your outline and essay, treat each group as a separate paragraph with its own "point-to-be-discussed" statement (in the outline) and topic sentence (in the body of the essay). Also include a simple TITLE, an INTRODUCTORY PARAGRAPH (that announces what the essay will be about), and a CONCLUDING PARAGRAPH (that brings the essay to an end, often by making some important point relative to its topic). Make your description as complete and accurate as possible, and rely just as much on the helpfulness of your comparisons as on the exactness of your physical descriptions. For the paragraphs with topic sentences, follow the directions for both the outlining and the writing—as far as they apply—that you were given in Practices N and P.

Chapter 11

Front Wording

Practice A: IDENTIFYING FRONT ADVERBIALS

[From text, page 187]

Directions: For each of these sentences, TEST THE WORDING BEFORE THE COMMA TO SEE IF YOU CAN SHIFT IT TO THE END OF THE SENTENCE UNIT. **IF YOU CAN**, label the front wording with a PAIR OF ARROWHEADS, **and** place the lettering **FAV** placed over the first arrowhead. **IF YOU CANNOT**, LEAVE THE SENTENCE UNLABELED. Imitate the examples.

FAV

Examples: ⟨If it rains⟩, shouldn't we plan to go ahead anyway?

The swift , darting , graceful birds were everywhere.

1. Because baldness is an inherited trait , someone with a thick head of hair could easily lose it prematurely.

2. After the lamp shade was hit by the flying toy , the light bulb was visible through the new hole.

3. The lack of one headlight , the mist , and the non-existence of a center dividing line made the early morning ride dangerous.

4. Since daylight savings time has started earlier in the spring , valuable amounts of electricity are now being conserved.

5. If I raised my hand , would she get angry?

6. An electrical blackout , which now rarely occurs , can create panic.

Practice B: Labeling Verbs inside Front Adverbials

[From text, page 187]

Directions: For each of the sentences in Practice A that has a front adverbial, FIND AND LABEL ANY VERBS THAT ARE **INSIDE** THE FRONT ADVERBIAL. **Use the TWO verb tests.** Imitate the example.

Example: FAV ⟨If it [does rain] ^rains⟩, shouldn't we plan to go ahead anyway?

Practice C: Taking Note of Commas

[From text, page 189]

Directions: For each of these sentences, just CIRCLE ITS COMMA.

Example: When you pay another a compliment (,) you make that person's day.

1. When a car has no snow tires , a driver must be extra cautious.
2. When the air is cold , a football stings one's hands in an unexpected way.
3. If a grade is below passing , shouldn't you be most angry at yourself?
4. When the temperature nears freezing in the North , can't the South be enjoying mild weather?
5. Though the ground was covered with small branches , the nearby trees did not seem unhealthy.
6. When several warm days follow each other , don't plants flourish?

Practice D: LABELING FRONT ADVERBIAL WORDING CORRECTLY

[From text, page 189]

Directions: For the sentences in Practice C, **TEST FOR FRONT ADVERBIAL WORDING.** If you find a front adverbial, label it with a pair of ARROWHEADS **and** the lettering FAV over the first arrowhead. Imitate the example.

Example: FAV ⟨When soda strikes a keyboard⟩, electrical circuits malfunction.

Practice E: DETERMINING WHETHER FRONT WORDING IS OR IS NOT A FRONT ADVERBIAL

[From text, page 190]

Directions: For each of these sentences, **TEST WHETHER THE WORDING BEFORE THE COMMA IS A FRONT ADVERBIAL.** Whenever it is, label it with a pair of ARROWHEADS and the lettering FAV as usual. Otherwise, leave the sentence unlabeled.

1. After the invention of the fluorescent light , regular light bulbs were rarely seen in offices.
2. For a change , couldn't the grades be passed around in the other direction?
3. The light , soothing breeze offset the heavy , midday heat.
4. Thomas O'Leary , an Irishman with a will to work , has done much carpentry work for my father .
5. When hunters are prowling the forests , people who like to stroll should have sense enough to stay at home.
6. After my chores were over , I played football with my friends.

Practice F: CARRYING OUT THE COMMA TEST, MAIN SUBJECT TEST—FOR QUESTIONS, AND THE TWO VERB TESTS

[From text, page 192]

Directions: For these sentences, CARRY OUT THE COMMA TEST, QUESTION MARK TEST, AND THE TWO VERB TESTS (TESTS 1–4) ONLY. Imitate the example.

Example: FAV ⟨If Jan ^needs [does need] a reminder⟩, shouldn't (MS) ⌈we⌉ (S) ^call [should] her?

1. When the sun rises , is the sky always pink?

2. If someone asks more questions , doesn't more education take place?

3. When a window is open , doesn't a person stay more alert?

4. If they took more notes , wouldn't students remember material longer?

5. If you have enjoyed one book , couldn't you find many more books to enjoy?

6. If a computer misbehaves , is the remedy always expensive?

Practice G: CARRYING OUT ALL TESTS

[From text, page 195]

Directions: For these sentences, CARRY OUT TESTS 1–6 IN FULL.

Though you can see birds through a window , the birds often can't see you. Phil Jacobs , a neighbor of mine , has watched cardinals stare him in the eye without their knowing it. Unless I am mistaken , this is why birds sometimes fly into people's windows. Since the bird sees its own image , the bird is sure that what it sees is an intruder. A scientist , who is a friend of mine , shared this information with me. If a bird should look at your window , it will often see a reflection of itself.

Practice H: CARRYING OUT ALL TESTS

[From text, page 196]

Directions: For these sentences, **CARRY OUT TESTS 1–6 IN FULL**.

1. Through the help of reminders , students can more easily meet deadlines at school.

2. When our emotions control our behavior , do we behave in ways that we are proud of?

3. Clear , crisp fall days give hints of a cooling trend.

4. If you don't place a stamp on a letter , will the letter come back to you?

5. When you do some homework each day , doesn't the work seem easier?

6. Since a plan is a help to a writer , an outline should always come first.

Practice J: TELLING FRONT ADVERBIALS FROM MAIN SUBJECTS IN SENTENCES WITHOUT A COMMA

[From text, page 197]

Directions: For these sentences, CARRY OUT TESTS 1–6 IN FULL. **Expect to find front adverbials that have no comma following them.** Imitate the example.

Example: ⟨For a few moments⟩ ^[did] Ⓢ the sky ^[did sparkle] MS sparkled with lightning. [?] (FAV)

1. After supper we often play card games.

2. Fridays the school day does not seem as long.

3. In some advertisements the unsuspecting can be easily deceived.

4. For quite a while we could hear the distant hooting of an owl.

5. Last year the brook by our house overflowed its banks.

6. Occasionally a man will not wear his favorite sweater.

Practice K: IDENTIFYING FRONT ADVERBIALS IN STATEMENTS WITH AND WITHOUT COMMAS

[From text, page 197]

Directions: For these sentences, **CARRY OUT TESTS 1–6 IN FULL.**

1. In a few minutes the noon whistle will be sounding.

2. For those who count calories , diet soda may taste better than no soda.

3. Laughter , which always refreshes a person , is something that is never in

   too great supply.

4. In near-thirty weather the boys were playing basketball out-of-doors.

5. His parents , brother , and sister would always spend a week in the

   mountains.

6. With spectacular speed a cat springs toward its prey.

Practice L: CARRYING OUT ALL THE TESTS

[From text, page 197]

Directions: For these sentences, **CARRY OUT TESTS 1–6 IN FULL.**

1. Due to mindless memorizing , Sally flunked the test.

2. By all rights a coach should give every player some playing time.

3. Whether it would resume snowing before nightfall was still unforeseeable.

4. By late spring , students get restless and flighty.

5. If I had studied with more concentration , wouldn't I have remembered more on the test?

6. His having taken detailed notes on everything said in class helped Ed receive the highest grade in the class.

7. Despite its coughing motor the boat lasted until it reached the dock.

8. Haltingly the wary swimmers inched their way into the frigid water.

Practice M: REWORDING SENTENCES WITH A SINGLE SWITCH WHEN TESTING FOR FRONT ADVERBIALS

[From text, page 198]

Directions: For each of these sentences, SHIFT THE FRONT WORDING TO THE END **and make the appropriate changes in the nouns and pronouns**.

Example: When a fluorescent light is dying, it lights up less quickly ➡

A fluorescent light lights up less quickly when it is dying.

1. When a player learns a sport while young , he has an advantage over others.

____

____

2. If our highways had no billboards , they would be more picturesque.

____

3. When a rabbit leaves tracks in the snow , it gives away its location.

____

4. When a person waits until the last minute , he/she makes unnecessary mistakes.

____

5. When the song birds return , they announce the return of spring.

____

6. If lightning strikes a building , it causes much mischief.

____

Practice N: CARRYING OUT LABELING USING ALL TESTS

[From text, page 198]

Directions: For these sentences, **CARRY OUT TESTS 1–6 IN FULL. Do any necessary rewording in your head only.**

1. If your bike has a soft tire , you cannot steer it as easily.

2. If you have saved quizzes , you can use them for review.

3. Though a book has small print , it might have important content.

4. When you transplant a tree , you must give it fertilizer.

5. If you wash dishes daily , you do not have stacks of them lying around.

6. When a person constantly forgets things , he/she must create reminders.

Practice P: CARRYING OUT ALL THE TESTS

[From text, page 198]

Directions: For these sentences, **CARRY OUT TESTS 1–6 IN FULL. Do any needed rewording in your head.**

1. Since the mare was finding hay to nibble on , she was no longer breaking her fence.

2. Oftentimes something improvised can serve the same purpose as something bought.

3. Since some games require a familiarity with words , they are enjoyed most by those who do a fair amount of reading.

4. Even in winter , won't a small amount of sunshine provide a lot of heat for a solar-heated home?

5. When people rise before dawn , they feel that they have gained extra time.

6. Though midwinter had a warm spell , it did not stay warm.

Practice Q: Rewording Sentences with Pairs of Switches when Testing for Front Adverbial Wording

[From text, page 199]

Directions: For each of these sentences, SHIFT THE FRONT WORDING TO THE END **and make the appropriate changes in the nouns and pronouns**.

1. When you ship belongings in a wooden box, it protects them.

   ____

2. If you expose documents to too much sunlight, it can ruin them.

   ____

3. If Tom had made breakfast for himself, he could have eaten it earlier.

   ____

4. If Jane had owned some erasing fluid, she could have used it to erase her errors.

   ____

5. If Bill could remember where he places his tools, he could use them to finish more jobs.

   ____

   ____

6. Whenever people make a list of grocery items needed, they can use it to prevent their running out of things.

   ____

   ____

Practice R: CARRYING OUT LABELING USING ALL TESTS

[From text, page 199]

Directions: For these sentences, CARRY OUT TESTS 1–6 IN FULL. **Do any necessary rewording in your head.**

1. Since Ruth has her own dictionary , she uses it often.
2. Though Paul saves magazines , he never rereads them.
3. Though the lake has fish , it seems to hide them.
4. When Jim broke his sled , he tried to fix it.
5. If a hawk spies a mouse , it dives after it.
6. Though the ice clung to the branches , it did not break them.

Practice S: CARRYING OUT ALL THE TESTS

[From text, page 199]

Directions: For these sentences, CARRY OUT TESTS 1–6 IN FULL. **Do any necessary rewording in your head.**

1. Though a warm spell has replaced the more usual February weather , it will not last indefinitely.
2. Despite Jane's fear of heights , she has learned to ski down scary slopes.
3. When Jim remembered what he had done with his lunch money , he could not believe that he had left it behind.
4. When lightning strikes a TV's booster , it ruins it utterly.
5. If people ride bikes , shouldn't they ride them on the right side of the road?
6. When the moisture sealed the envelopes , it made them almost worthless.

Practice T: Rewording Sentences Requiring More Complicated Switching when Testing for Front Adverbials

[From text, page 200]

Directions: For each of these sentences, SHIFT THE FRONT WORDING TO THE END **and make all the appropriate and required changes. Take your time.** YOU MUST OFTEN DO MAJOR REWORDING.

1. Though the repairman had promised to arrive on Tuesday, that day ended with no sign of his arrival.

 ____

 ____

2. If a nonswimmer is in a boat that capsizes, he must hold onto any part of the boat he can reach.

 ____

 ____

3. When a bird that has a black mask across its face gets the name "yellow-throated warbler," its name-giver must have observed it at too great a distance.

 ____

 ____

 ____

4. When a busy person has made a list of things to do, he/she must not forget to consult it.

 ____

 ____

5. When a writer is searching for a word, he/she can often find it in a thesaurus.

 ____

 ____

6. Though our dog first grabs a stick as he accompanies his master, he is quickly distracted by any sign of something else's presence.

 ____

 ____

Practice U: CARRYING OUT LABELING USING ALL TESTS

[From text, page 201]

Directions: For the sentences in this passage, **CARRY OUT ALL THE TESTS (AND STEPS) TO FOLLOW TO SUCCEED—NAMELY, TESTS 1–6**.

Three Weeks to Success

As I recall , the article I read was in the *Reader's Digest* about three years ago. In it , the author told how quickly new habits take root. Hadn't she found that it takes only three weeks?

Since those who succeed at schoolwork are those who do the right things regularly, my recommendation is that students begin by sticking to improved study practices for three weeks. For example , students must learn to live by a time chart that provides enough study time for each subject. In addition , don't students need to form the habit of previewing chapters before reading them? Without question , students must also write out in some shortened way whatever material they are expected to know.

Practice V: CARRYING OUT ALL THE TESTS

[From text, page 201]

Directions: For the sentences in this passage, **CARRY OUT TESTS 1–6 IN FULL.**

Keeping Records

When you think about it , do you remember what you hear in class long? There have been studies on this. In these studies researchers discovered that students remember only 20% of material heard. Doesn't this surprise you? Can a person who wants to remember things longer achieve this? When students are smart , they put everything that they must know in writing. As a result of this , they always have something to fall back on.

Practice W: CARRYING OUT ALL THE TESTS

[From text, page 201]

Directions: For the sentences in this passage, **CARRY OUT TESTS 1–6 IN FULL**.

Preventing Forgetting

There are other ways to help yourself remember longer. First of all , you must fully digest what you want to remember. You do this by making an outline in your own words.

Ideally , this outline should have headings before each section that explain its category of importance. A category of importance is a word like "advantages," "differences," or "reasons."

After you have your outline , you must recall the content often enough that you will never forget more than 15% of the material. If your outline has ingrained the content on your mind , this should require only occasional reviews.

Practice X: Writing Sentences with Front Adverbials

[From text, page 204]

Directions: WRITE **EIGHT** SENTENCES OF YOUR OWN THAT HAVE FRONT ADVERBIALS. **Be sure to use a comma to separate the front adverbial from the main part of the sentence.** Imitate the example.

Example: When you see colorful blossoms in rich display**,** you know that spring has arrived.

PARAGRAPH AND ESSAY SUPPLEMENT
COMPARISON

GOAL IN THIS MINI-CHAPTER

To practice writing effective paragraphs developed by comparison.

PARAGRAPH BY COMPARISON

A paragraph by COMPARISON is a paragraph in which you compare or contrast the likenesses or differences between persons or things. Such paragraphs have the benefits of making your point clearer to readers, more concrete, and more persuasive (when that is your objective).

PRACTICE Y: PLANNING A PARAGRAPH DEVELOPED BY COMPARISON

DIRECTIONS: Write out a somewhat general comparison that you can "prove" by adding specific details. Then list the details that support your general statement. State both the general comparison and each detail of the comparison in the simplest English possible—use the *-er* ending for a word or the word *more* before it (as in *Carlos is tall**ER** than Bill* and *Barb is **MORE** athletic than her sister*). Imitate the example outline supplied below.

Example Outline

USING ABBREVIATIONS AS YOU TAKE NOTES IS BETTER THAN WRITING WORDS OUT IN FULL

You can include more material.
You have more time to listen.
You have more material to study from.
You have more self-confidence on tests.
You have more material to ask questions about.
You have more to compare with what is in the text.

Practice Z: WRITING A PARAGRAPH DEVELOPED BY COMPARISON

DIRECTIONS: Write a paragraph based on the outline you prepared for Practice Y. Make sure that you use as much repetition and echoing as the subject matter requires. Also be consistent in your use of pronoun reference and tenses. Moreover, you should use signpost wording to guide your reader through your listing. Imitate the example paragraph supplied below.

Example Paragraph

STUDENTS WHO USE ABBREVIATIONS TAKE NOTES BETTER THAN THOSE WHO DO NOT. *First, those who use abbreviations write down more of what a teacher says or writes than does someone who writes out every letter. Moreover, those who abbreviate have more time to hear a teacher's additional explanations than those who do not abbreviate. In addition, those who abbreviate tend to have fuller notes to study from than do those who write out every word. Finally, those who use abbreviations are less frustrated than those who write out everything and fail to keep up or are always uncomfortably far behind.* [Notice how this is a two-sided comparison—that is, something is said about both types of students in every sentence (alternatively, side-by-side sentences could have been used to achieve the same effect). You should do the same.]

Practice AA: PLANNING AND WRITING ANOTHER PARAGRAPH DEVELOPED BY COMPARISON

DIRECTIONS: Follow the directions of Practices Y and Z, and write another paragraph of comparison but with different subject matter.

Practice BB: PLANNING AND WRITING AN ESSAY DEVELOPED BY COMPARISON ALONE

DIRECTIONS: Prepare both an outline and an essay that compare two persons, types of places (such as vacation spots, schools, houses, and so forth), or types of activities (such as different sports, different musical instruments, different recreational activities, and so forth) IN SEVERAL RESPECTS OR AREAS—EACH OF WHICH YOU CAN WRITE A SEPARATE PARAGRAPH ABOUT. For example, you can compare two people according to their school accomplishments, athletic abilities, interests, character, and/or personality. Write an outline and an essay that use each AREA of difference as the source of a new topic sentence and set of comparisons. Also include a simple TITLE for your essay, an INTRODUCTION (a paragraph that announces the areas of comparison to be treated), and a CONCLUSION (a paragraph that summarizes, analyzes causes, predicts the future, or points to some lesson to be learned). For the paragraphs with topic sentences, follow the directions for both the outlining and the writing—as far as they apply—that were given in Practices Y and Z.

Chapter 12

Introduction to Conjunctions and Punctuation

Practice A: Punctuating Joined Predicates

[From text, page 215]

Directions: Combine each pair of sentences **into two predicates joined by a coordinating conjunction, but use NO internal punctuation** (the right conjunction has been supplied for you). Imitate the example.

Example: [BUT] The dog braved the snow on the way to the mailbox.
He retreated back into the house quickly upon returning.

The dog braved the snow on the way to the mailbox **but** retreated back into the house quickly upon returning.

[BUT] The sun would break out of the clouds.
The sun would quickly hide again.

____

____

[AND] The driver put on his seat belt.
He started the car.

____

[OR] A student will guess at a word's meaning.
He/she will look it up in a dictionary.

____

____

[BUT] The days get longer after December 21st.
The days seem just as long until mid-January.

____

____

[AND] Sally took out two pens.
She opened her notebook.

____

Practice B: Writing One's Own Sentences with Properly Joined Predicates

[From text, page 215]

Directions: Write three sentences of your own in which you **join two predicates** (verbs and words that belong just with them) **by means of a coordinating conjunction and no comma**.

____

____

____

Practice C: Punctuating Joined Sentence Units

[From text, page 216]

Directions: Combine the same pairs of sentences that you did in Practice A, but combine them into **two sentence units**. Use **first** a comma and **then** a conjunction (the conjunction has been supplied for you). Imitate the example.

Example: [BUT] The dog braved the snow on the way to the mailbox.
He retreated back into the house quickly upon returning.

The dog braved the snow on the way to the mailbox**, but** he retreated back into the house quickly upon returning.

[BUT] The sun would break out of the clouds.
The sun would quickly hide again.

____

[AND] The driver put on his seat belt.
He started the car.

____

[OR] A student will guess at a word's meaning.
He/she will look it up in a dictionary.

____

____

[BUT] The days get longer after December 21st.
The days seem just as long until mid-January.

____

____

[AND] The student sharpened her pencils.
She opened her notebook.

____

Practice D: WRITING ONE'S OWN SENTENCES WITH PROPERLY JOINED SENTENCE UNITS

[From text, page 216]

DIRECTIONS: WRITE THREE SENTENCES OF YOUR OWN in which you **JOIN TWO SENTENCE UNITS** by means of **both** a COMMA **and** a later COORDINATING CONJUNCTION.

____

____

____

____

____

____

Practice E: PUNCTUATING SENTENCES THAT CONTAIN A SERIES

[From text, page 217]

DIRECTIONS: COMBINE THESE SENTENCES IN THE SIMPLEST WAY POSSIBLE. **Punctuate the series correctly.** Imitate the example.

Example: The coach picked Ed Sam and me for the team.

The coach picked Ed**,** Sam**,** and me for the team.

1. Mom gives us corn flakes granola and 40% bran flakes for breakfast.
2. A shovel a pick and brute strength were needed.
3. People read books for enjoyment information and instruction.
4. Peas broccoli and spinach are my favorite vegetables.
5. Sun salt and scraping remove ice from walkways.
6. For a camp fire, prepare a place out of the wind an area free of flammable items and an area without overhanging branches.

Practice F: Writing Sentences of Your Own That Contain a Series

[From text, page 217]

Directions: Write, and punctuate correctly, three sentences of your own **that contain a series**—that is, that contain three or more grammatical elements joined by commas and a coordinating conjunction. Imitate the example sentence in Practice E above.

____

____

____

Practice G: Using a Semi-colon to Join Two Sentence Units

[From text, page 218]

Directions: Combine these pairs of sentences into one. **Use just a semi-colon to separate/join them**, and **change the capital letter of the second to a lower-case letter**. Imitate the example.

Example: Mom is away. My Dad is coping.

Mom is away**;** **m**y Dad is coping.

1. Some chairs withstand the roughhousing of teenagers. Other chairs collapse.

   ____

2. Sometimes the mailman arrives really early. Other times he arrives really late.

   ____

3. A homeowner can do things that a carpenter does. The carpenter does them quicker and better.

   ____

4. The hurried reader reads to finish a book. The unhurried reader reads to absorb the book.

   ____

   ____

5. Homeowners at high altitudes have cooler summers. They also have cooler winters.

   ____

6. To the optimist, the clouds are lessening. To the pessimist, they are still thickening.

   ____

Practice H: USING A SEMI-COLON AND TRANSITIONAL ADVERBIAL TO JOIN SENTENCES UNITS

[From text, page 219]

DIRECTIONS: COMBINE THESE PAIRS OF SENTENCES INTO ONE. **USE A SEMI-COLON AND A TRANSITIONAL ADVERBIAL (AT THE START OF THE SECOND) TO JOIN THEM.** Be sure to add a comma **after** the transitional adverbial. Choices of possible transitional adverbs have been added before each sentence. **Note that you must choose the one that makes most sense in the context of the sentence.** Imitate the example.

Example: [IN ADDITION, THEREFORE, NONETHELESS] There was no let-up in the rain. The forecast was for sunshine to take its place.

There was no let-up in the rain**; nonetheless,** the forecast was for sunshine to take its place.

1. [IN ADDITION, THEREFORE, NONETHELESS] The blue jays flew in. A flock of geese were arriving.

   ____

2. [IN ADDITION, THEREFORE, NONETHELESS] Everyone looks forward to mail. Many receive what they are looking for.

   ____

3. [IN ADDITION, THEREFORE, NONETHELESS] Honey sweetens food. It sweetens the fingers that can't get away from it.

   ____

4. [NEVERTHELESS, THEREFORE, MOREOVER] To some people, money is for hording. To others, money is for sharing.

   ____

5. [NEVERTHELESS, THEREFORE, MOREOVER] Homeowners loathe the mice that seek warmth in winter. Cats cherish them.

   ____

6. [NEVERTHELESS, THEREFORE, MOREOVER] Some people count the days that have not come. Others count the days that have come.

   ____

   ____

7. [NEVERTHELESS, THEREFORE, MOREOVER] A dictionary tells you all the meanings that a particular word carries. A thesaurus tells you all the words that carry a particular meaning.

   ____

   ____

Practice J: Joining Two Sentence Units by Changing One to a Dependent Clause

[From text, page 219]

Directions: Combine these pairs of sentence units into one. **Use the introducer** (supplied in brackets) **to change one of the pairs**—the one for which it makes most sense—**to a dependent clause.** Note the Example.

Example: [THOUGH] Some writers hate revising. Other writers cannot revise enough.

Though some writers hate revising**,** others cannot revise enough.

1. [THOUGH] The horses whinnied for their breakfast. The caretaker was still asleep.

2. [BECAUSE] The barn started slipping off its foundation. The farmer had to sell his cows.

3. [BECAUSE] The supporting poles were placed closer together. The power lines were thicker and heavier.

4. [BECAUSE] The mailman arrived early. I missed my chance to mail a letter.

5. [THOUGH] The Thanksgiving Day service began at 9:30 a.m. A surprising number of church members attended.

6. [THOUGH] The young horse had jumped over the gate. She squeezed through the two strands of barbed wire to get back in.

7. [THOUGH] The sky was cloudless. The temperature never rose above 30 degrees.

8. [BECAUSE] Joe could not open his locker. He had misplaced his key.

Practice K: CHANGING FRAGMENTS TO SENTENCES

[From text, page 221]

DIRECTIONS: For all these groups of words, **CARRY OUT ENOUGH OF THE TESTS**—at least the two verb tests and the Movable Starter Test—**TO DETERMINE WHICH ONES ARE ALREADY SENTENCES**. For those that **are** sentences, leave the **blank space empty**. For those that are **not** sentences, **add enough words** so that they become acceptable sentences. Imitate the example.

Example: [SENTENCE / FRAGMENT] When the sun comes out

When the sun comes out, SNOW STARTS DISAPPEARING.
[or] EVERYONE IS CHEERED when the sun comes out.

1. [SENTENCE / FRAGMENT] When Tom lost a glove in the snow

___

2. [SENTENCE / FRAGMENT] Whoever owns it should speak up

___

3. [SENTENCE / FRAGMENT] Since people saw it without realizing what it was

___

4. [SENTENCE / FRAGMENT] Getting himself in worse trouble by lying

___

5. [SENTENCE / FRAGMENT] With no time left for double checking

___

6. [SENTENCE / FRAGMENT] Nothing ever came of Al's suggestion for saving time

___

7. [SENTENCE / FRAGMENT] At the end of the road that is called "Lincoln Avenue"

___

8. [SENTENCE / FRAGMENT] By listening to music while trying to do an assignment

___

9. [SENTENCE / FRAGMENT] Though afraid that she might not be able to put her question into words

___

___

10. [SENTENCE / FRAGMENT] Opening presents early can become a habit

___

Practice L: Remedying Comma Splices

[From text, page 222]

Directions: Each of these sentences has three dots that separate two sentence units and show the place where you may **not** place a comma but **must make some change**. COMBINE THESE PAIRS OF SENTENCE UNITS IN THE WAY YOU FEEL WOULD BEST HELP THE READER—usually this will require the addition of at least one word. **Be sure to use correct punctuation and appropriate wording.** (You may also need to add a capital letter.)

1. The temperature remained near freezing ... the air kept feeling colder.

____

____

2. Mom and Dad took turns building the doll house ... we children took turns helping.

____

____

3. The roads at the higher elevations were icy ... the main roads were ice-free.

____

____

4. Users of seat belts are sometimes unharmed in severe accidents ... Non-users are sometimes harmed in minor accidents.

____

____

5. A vacation is a time to relax ... it is not a time to continue working just as hard as you were.

____

____

6. The ads you receive emphasize what you can receive free ... they never emphasize what must eventually be anything but "free."

____

____

Practice M: COMBINING PAIRS OF SENTENCE UNITS CORRECTLY

[From text, page 223]

DIRECTIONS: This passage has no punctuation. CHANGE THE PASSAGE IN ALL THE WAYS NECESSARY AND APPROPRIATE TO MAKE IT AS READABLE AS POSSIBLE. **Feel free to ADD WORDING (or substitute your wording for a word like *and*) to improve clearness and/or readability. Add correct punctuation.**

Frank wanted to use the house's TV antenna to increase the number of channels he could receive on his radio he decided to try to attach the antenna from his radio to the antenna of the TV he suddenly got the bright idea to attach his antenna to the power pack that enables the booster to work he shorted the transformer in the power pack and he caused the loss of TV reception in the house until the transformer could be replaced and this took three weeks and these weeks included the whole week of Thanksgiving vacation and his brothers and sisters not to mention his parents were far less than grateful.

* * * * *

PARAGRAPH AND ESSAY SUPPLEMENT
DEFINITION/CLARIFICATION

GOAL IN THIS MINI-CHAPTER

To practice writing paragraphs that "define" by clarifying what you mean.

PARAGRAPH BY DEFINITION/CLARIFICATION

A paragraph by DEFINITION/CLARIFICATION is a paragraph that clarifies for the reader exactly what you do and do not mean by some term related to your topic. The "definition" in question is NEVER a dictionary definition; it is, rather, an informal CLARIFICATION of what the term you are using means for the purposes of your paragraph or essay. This kind of paragraph has special importance in persuasive essays and in some informative essays.

Practice N: PLANNING A PARAGRAPH DEVELOPED BY DEFINITION/CLARIFICATION

DIRECTIONS: Think of a topic that you have strong feelings about—and might want to write an essay about. The topic could be friendship, exercise, sportsmanship, courteousness, pricing, commercials, smog, and so forth. Write out what you mean by the term in a brief statement. Then, in outline form, list—for someone else's sake—both what you **do** mean by the term (that is, all the features and/or characteristics that you are including) and what you do **not** mean. (It makes no difference whether you discuss what you do mean first or what you do not mean.) Now turn this "outline" into a paragraph by definition/clarification. Imitate the example outline supplied below.

Example Outline

NOTE-TAKING IS THE CAPTURING OF THE CONTENTS OF A LECTURE ON PAPER

Included: introductions, conclusions, asides, examples, written statements

Excluded: absolutely nothing that happens during a lecture that is relevant to the subject matter and could conceivably influence one's grade for a course

Also excluded: writing done after the lecture is over at one's desk when studying

Practice P: WRITING A PARAGRAPH DEVELOPED BY DEFINITION/CLARIFICATION

DIRECTIONS: Write a paragraph based on the outline you prepared for Practice N. Make sure that you use as much repetition and echoing as the subject matter requires. Also be consistent in your use of pronoun reference and tenses. Imitate the example paragraph supplied below.

Example Paragraph

THE TERM "NOTE-TAKING," AS I USE IT HERE, MEANS THE CAPTURING ON A PAGE OF THE ENTIRE CONTENT OF A TEACHER'S LECTURE—IN READABLE WRITING. *It includes everything said or written that could have a bearing on a grade for a course—whether in an introduction, a reference, an aside, or an example. On the other hand, it excludes any note-taking that a student might do after a class is over or at a desk later in the day. In other words, it is a verbatim capturing of everything said or written by a teacher during class time, as far as that is humanly or reasonably possible.*

Practice Q: PLANNING AND WRITING ANOTHER PARAGRAPH DEVELOPED BY DEFINITION/CLARIFICATION

DIRECTIONS: Write a paragraph on a different topic—such as, possibly, what you do and do not mean by jogging, cooking, reading, studying, or practicing. Follow all the directions given in Practices N and P above.

Chapter 13

Questions That Start with a Question Word

Practice A: Labeling Starter-Verb Questions

[From text, page 239]

Directions: For these sentences, carry out the Comma Test and the Main Subject Test—for Questions through Step III, A. Imitate the example.

Example: ⟨If you live in the country⟩, can you get cable TV? (FAV over "If"; MS over "can"; Ⓢ over "you"; [can] inserted before "get")

1. In winter , isn't the sun lower in the sky?

2. Didn't Joan volunteer again?

3. If a walkway has been shoveled , isn't it less dangerous.

4. When events of importance happen , the networks interrupt TV programs.

5. Could a clock that is fast cause undue panic?

6. Doesn't a farmer who quits farming discard a unique way of living?

Practice B: LABELING THE MOVABLE STARTER IN QUESTION-WORD QUESTIONS

[From text, page 239]

DIRECTIONS: For these sentences, CARRY OUT THE COMMA TEST AND THE MAIN SUBJECT TEST—FOR QUESTIONS THROUGH STEP III, B, 1. Imitate the examples.

Example: FAV ⟨After summer vacation is over⟩, when MS will lessons begin?

Whose book ^ MS [did fall] fell in the mud?

1. In winter , where do ants go?

2. Why aren't we assigned more homework?

3. Whose sled has been left in the snow?

4. If a fire starts , what should a person do first?

5. Which of the clocks has the most accurate time?

6. At night time , who is in charge of locking up?

Practice C: TESTING WHETHER A STARTER CAN SHIFT TO THE RIGHT

[From text, page 240]

DIRECTIONS: For each of the sentences in Practice B, TEST WHETHER THE MOVABLE STARTER CAN SHIFT TO THE RIGHT. IF IT CAN, **reposition it there**. Imitate the examples.

Example: FAV ⟨After summer vacation is over⟩, when MS will lessons ^[will] begin?

Whose book ^ MS [did fall] fell in the mud? [Supplied *did* cannot shift.]

Practice D: CARRYING OUT THE COMMA TEST AND THE MAIN SUBJECT TEST—FOR QUESTIONS (EXPANDED) THROUGH STEP III, B, 2, A, ④

[From text, page 241]

DIRECTIONS: For these sentences, CARRY OUT THE COMMA TEST AND THE MAIN SUBJECT TEST FOR QUESTIONS THROUGH STEPS III, B, 2, A, ④. Imitate the example.

Example: FAV ⟨If they add a new electric line⟩, ⟨where⟩ MS will Ⓢ they ^[will] run it?

1. Why didn't they give us a "snow day" today?

2. When it rains hard , where does all the rain go?

3. If a person is good at science , why can't he/she be good at English?

4. When you want to pay less for something , where can you go?

5. How do students who are most successful study?

6. If you do not know , how soon could you find out?

Practice E: MORE CARRYING OUT OF THE COMMA TEST AND THE MAIN SUBJECT TEST—FOR QUESTIONS THROUGH STEP III, B, 2, A, ④

[From text, page 241]

DIRECTIONS: CARRY OUT THE SAME DIRECTIONS AS FOR PRACTICE D, **but expect both STARTER-VERB QUESTIONS and QUESTION-WORD QUESTIONS.**

1. If we have packing snow , couldn't we build a tunnel?

2. When tests come , why do some people forget what they studied?

3. When is a word processor not better than a typewriter?

4. Isn't skill at keyboarding a requirement for enjoyment of word processing?

5. If your desk faced the west , wouldn't you see the pretty sunsets?

6. How often does a good writer make changes in what he has written?

Practice F: WRITING QUESTIONS WHOSE MOVABLE STARTER SHIFTS TO THE RIGHT

[From text, page 241]

DIRECTIONS: On the blank lines supplied, WRITE THREE SHORT QUESTION-WORD QUESTIONS OF YOUR OWN **in which the movable starter can shift to the right**. The question word wording has been supplied for you. Imitate the example.

Example: HOW LATE will the train be? [You can shift *will* to before *be*: *the train will be how late*]

Which pages ______________________________

Whose pen ______________________________

How many paragraphs ______________________________

Practice G: CARRYING OUT ALL TESTS

[From text, page 242]

DIRECTIONS: For these sentences, CARRY OUT ALL THE TESTS AND STEPS. **Be sure to label all remaining verbs, especially inside front adverbials.**

1. As you look at a page , which position catches your eye first?
2. In spring , what kinds of things can clog a brook?
3. Which person in the class should ask the most questions?
4. If something cooks too long , what happens?
5. What driver would not fix the headlights if he/she knew that the one on the driver's side was out?
6. When dinner is cooking , whose stomach doesn't respond?

Practice H: CARRYING OUT ALL TESTS

[From text, page 242]

DIRECTIONS: For these sentences, CARRY OUT ALL THE TESTS AND STEPS. **Note that both kinds of Question-Word Questions will be intermixed.**

1. When you need new batteries , which kind truly lasts longest?
2. If a house uses wood heat , how often should its flue be cleared?
3. Which brand of paper towels has outperformed all others?
4. In winter , where do squirrels disappear to?
5. When TV stations take an ad "break," how long do you think they last?
6. If you want peak mental alertness , how much exercise is ideal?

Practice J: CARRYING OUT ALL TESTS

[From text, page 242]

DIRECTIONS: For these sentences, CARRY OUT ALL THE TESTS AND STEPS. **Note that both Starter-Verb Questions and Question-Word Questions will be intermixed.**

1. When a cat is friendly , who can be angry at it?
2. When the ground is covered with snow , aren't the days brighter?
3. For the best mileage , how fast should a person drive his/her car?
4. What creature is more playful than a kitten?
5. If a rubber band is too short , can't you attach two rubber bands together?
6. How long might a pretty sunset last?

Practice K: WRITING QUESTIONS WHOSE MOVABLE STARTER CAN <u>NOT</u> SHIFT TO THE RIGHT

[From text, page 242]

DIRECTIONS: On the blank lines supplied, WRITE THREE SHORT QUESTION-WORD QUESTIONS OF YOUR OWN **in which the movable starter can NOT shift to the right**. The question word wording has been supplied for you. Imitate the examples.

Examples: WHICH ANIMAL <u>pretends that it is dead?</u> [The supplied *does* can not shift to the right.]

WHOSE GLOVE <u>has fallen over there?</u> [*Has* cannot shift to the right.]

Which waste baskets ____

Whose bike ____

How many friends ____

Practice L: CARRYING OUT ALL THE TESTS

[From text, page 242]

DIRECTIONS: For these sentences, CARRY OUT ALL THE TESTS AND STEPS. Note that **because every kind of sentence has been intermixed**, you must **pay especially close attention to the type of end punctuation**.

1. How much a college education will cost cannot be easily determined.

2. How helpful an umbrella can be depends on the strength of the wind.

3. If you must eat between meals , what food is best for you?

4. When a dead branch is very high , how can a homeowner remove it?

5. When snow covers a road , there are many slippery places.

6. If a person is a careful driver , how safely can he/she drive in icy conditions?

7. In your opinion , which of the current TV programs are most worthwhile watching?

8. If you own a bicycle , what kind of oil should you use on it?

Practice M: CARRYING OUT ALL THE TESTS

[From text, page 242]

DIRECTIONS: For this passage, **CARRY OUT ALL THE TESTS (AND STEPS) TO FOLLOW TO SUCCEED BOTH FULLY AND IN THE CORRECT ORDER**.

"Freebies"

When you receive offers for something free in the mail , shouldn't you be suspicious? If you owned a business , how often would you give something away free? What business person would be such a fool?

When you receive a magazine "free," don't you also receive more and more issues for a specific amount of money? Doesn't the business expect that you will not cancel the subscription? How many people remember to write "cancel" across their bill? Whether you remember to do this determines whether your first issue is truly free.

How many "free" things worth owning have you ever received from an ad in the mail? If the number is zero , what choice can I give you other than that you should ignore the "free" offers as the hoaxes that they usually are.

Paragraph and Essay Supplement

Process

Goal in This Mini-Chapter

To practice writing process paragraphs and essays.

Paragraph by Process

A paragraph by PROCESS is a paragraph that simply lists the steps in a procedure—that is, in the carrying out of some objective. Such paragraphs have an important place in many informative and persuasive essays.

Practice N: Planning a Process Paragraph

Directions: Decide on some process to explain that has only a few simple steps. Then write out as your "point to be discussed" that this is the process that you will be explaining. In addition, list all the steps that make up the process to complete your outline—and arrange them in the right order. Imitate the example outline supplied below.

Example Outline

Steps to carry out as you preview a chapter
- *Read the title.*
- *Read the introduction.*
- *Preview each next paragraph:*
    - *Read its 1st sentence;*
    - *If necessary, read one more sentence;*
    - *If necessary, also read the last sentence.*
- *Read the whole conclusion.*

Practice P: WRITING A PROCESS PARAGRAPH

DIRECTIONS: Write a paragraph based on the outline you prepared for Practice N. Make sure that you use as much repetition and echoing as the subject matter requires. Also be consistent in your use of pronoun reference and tenses. Moreover, you must use signpost wording to reassure your readers that they are proceeding in the right order. Imitate the example paragraph supplied below.

Example Paragraph

THERE ARE STEPS TO FOLLOW TO MAKE YOUR PREVIEWING OF A CHAPTER OF A NONFICTION BOOK YIELD THE MOST POSSIBLE BENEFITS. *The first step is to read the title for any insight it might give to the author's attitude toward the subject. Second, read the introduction carefully, especially for clues to the author's plan for the chapter—that is, what the chapter's parts will be. (The introduction ends, by the way, when the author first starts to go back over something already said.) Third, preview every paragraph by reading fully and reflectively each first sentence—or, if that is not the topic sentence, the second sentence as well. If you still have not found a topic sentence, skip to the last sentence on the chance that it might contain a summary. The last step is to read the conclusion (that starts with wording like "in sum") in full. Now that you know the author's plan and the nature of the supporting details, you are ready to read the whole chapter to absorb and retain it.*

Practice Q: PLANNING AND WRITING A PROCESS ESSAY

DIRECTIONS: Decide on some process to explain that has groupings or stages of steps. Plan to make each grouping a paragraph by itself. Include in your plans a TITLE for the essay, an INTRODUCTION (a paragraph that announces what the whole essay is about), and a CONCLUSION (that informs readers that they know all there is to know to complete the process on their own **or** tells the readers something important relative to the topic). Then prepare an outline that has a topic statement for each inside paragraph. After that, make a list of all the necessary steps in each group and list them in the right order. Finally, write an essay that begins with an introduction, leads readers through all the steps in all the groups, and ends with a conclusion. Throughout your essay, use wording that assures your readers that they are proceeding in the right order.

Chapter 14

Subjects versus Objects

Practice A: CARRYING OUT TEST 1–7 THROUGH THE NONMAIN SUBJECT SUBTEST

[From text, page 255]

Directions: CARRY OUT TESTS 1–7—THROUGH THE NONMAIN SUBJECT SUBTEST. Imitate the example.

[does] Ⓢ MS [does plan]

Example: ^ Everybody [INT that S we have heard from] ^ plans on coming.

1. How could the single wire [INT that I had used] stop a horse ?

2. Is our young apple tree dying [because mice have attacked it] ?

3. [If you think about it] , a country setting lends beauty to a home .

4. Musical horns are still a rarity [because they are unappreciated] .

5. Who can sense temperature changes [when they happen gradually] ?

6. The country [INT that we live in] is rich in land and natural resources .

Practice B: Carrying out Tests 1–7 through the Nonmain Subject Subtest

[From text, page 255]

Directions: Follow the directions for Practice A.

Fall Chores

[When fall comes] , there are certain things INT [that a homeowner must do] . Shouldn't he first repair any faulty gutters ? [When that is done] , who could easily forget to also clear any fallen leaves out of the gutters ? Other chores abound [*exist in great number*] too . [If his pipes freeze] , why wouldn't a homeowner turn off the indoors faucet [where the water leaves the house] . [While he is at it] , he should also turn the corresponding out-of-doors faucet on INT [so the water can drain out] .

Practice C: CARRYING OUT TESTS 1–7, THROUGH THE OBJECT OF VERB SUBTEST

[From text, page 258]

Directions: CARRY OUT TESTS 1–7, **THROUGH THE OBJECT OF VERB SUBTEST**. Imitate the example.

Example: [do] ^Carpenter ants (S) [do love] ^love (MS) [to gnaw on houses [until they (S) [do destroy] ^destroy them (OV)]] (OV).

1. I have learned [that fish contain no fat] (INT).

2. Can't collected junk cause clutter?

3. Too few realize [why they should do a job right the first time].

4. What store owner wouldn't want to raise prices?

5. I noticed [that your guitar has a different kind of sound] (INT).

6. Why doesn't Carla share her book with Kim?

Practice D: CARRYING OUT TESTS 1–7, THROUGH THE OBJECT OF VERB SUBTEST

[From text, page 259]

Directions: FOLLOW THE DIRECTIONS FOR PRACTICE C.

Trespassers

[When a woodchuck raises its head by our house] , it is foolhardy [**not** an object of verb] . Why should our alert dog ignore so inquisitive an animal ? Wouldn't you resent large rodentlike animals [when they burrow holes at will on your master's turf] ? [If our Spike senses the presence of a woodchuck] , he races to the spot . With sinewy [*muscular*] speed , he pounces on the hapless [*luckless*] creature . He then relieves it of its life . [As you can well believe] , there are fewer woodchucks by our place now .

INT

Practice E: CARRYING OUT TESTS 1–7, THROUGH THE OBJECT OF VERB SUBTEST

[From text, page 259]

Directions: CARRY OUT THE DIRECTIONS FOR PRACTICE C.

A Secret Enemy

In how many ways can tiredness hurt the success of a student ? To begin with , doesn't lack of sleep slow the mind ? [If the mind works slower] , how much more studying must be done for the same results ? What student taking notes doesn't also use his mind ? [If his mind is in slow gear] , how can a student do this fast enough ? Also , wouldn't tired minds easily forget memorized material during tests ?

Practice F: IDENTIFYING PREPOSITIONS

[From text, page 263]

Directions: PLACE A RIGHT-ANGLE MARKER **around all the nine most important prepositions** in this passage. Imitate the example.

Example: The bird |with the sharp whistle has a home |at the top |of a willow tree.

When a woodchuck raises its head by our house , it is foolhardy . Why should our alert dog ignore so inquisitive an animal ? Wouldn't you resent large rodentlike animals when they burrow holes at will on your master's turf ? If our Spike senses the presence of a woodchuck , he races to the spot . With sinewy speed , he pounces on the hapless creature . He then relieves it of its life . As you can well believe , there are fewer woodchucks by our place now .

Practice G: CARRYING OUT TESTS 1–7, THROUGH THE PREPOSITION SUBTEST

[From text, page 264]

Directions: CARRY OUT TESTS 1–7—**THROUGH THE PREPOSITION SUBTEST**.

1. Don't most of us shed our winter coats with glee [after the warmth of spring arrives] ?

2. People in the South enjoy trips to the shore for a swim at almost all times of year .

3. Who wouldn't agree [that one's word to a friend is a pledge] ? (INT above "that")

4. A runner on first base must dash for second at the release of the ball on a hit-and-run play .

5. The echoing of voices in the mountains can surprise you with its clarity [if you pay attention to it] .

6. How often does the sound of the voice of someone on the phone interfere with your thought processes ?

Practice H: CARRYING OUT THE OBJECT OF PREPOSITION SUBTEST FOR TEST 7

[From text, page 265]

Directions: For the sentences in Practice G, FIND AND LABEL CORRECTLY **ALL OBJECTS OF PREPOSITIONS** (use an overhead bracket and the lettering OP). Imitate the example.

FAV — OP — OP — [did] Ⓢ

Example: ⟨At the signal from the starting gun⟩, ^ each runner

MS [did leap] — OP

^ leapt to his feet.

Practice J: Carrying out Tests 1–7 in Their Entirety

[From text, page 265]

Directions: For these sentences, CARRY OUT ALL THE TESTS (AND STEPS) TO FOLLOW TO SUCCEED THROUGH ALL OF TEST 7.

1. Didn't the pond at the top of the hill by your house have several large-mouthed bass of considerable size ?

2. An expedition from the country to New York City with a carful of children can cost a large amount of money .

3. [When items on the shelves in a store have been neatly arranged] , they easily catch the attention of curious on-lookers .

4. Buyers at auctions in the country could pay higher prices than [preposition] those at a store .

5. How many from the South lose their accent in time [if they do not often return there] ?

6. How late did the appraiser arrive on that cold day in the middle of May ?

Practice K: Carrying out Tests 1–7 in Their Entirety

[From text, page 265]

Directions: Follow the directions for Practice J.

Beach "Fun"

[Because everyone slept late] , the family of five left for the beach at eleven in the morning . Unfortunately , they brought two dogs and a cat .

Why wouldn't the crowds on the beach leave plenty of room for this lively group ? The two boys and the dogs raced for the water . Immediately , the parents and their daughter spread the blankets on the sand by their umbrella

INT [so they could be sheltered from the sun] . Could you believe INT [that the heat of the sun prevented sleeping on the part of anyone] ? In addition , what other cat would have discovered the food in the basket so quickly ? She had a great time with the sandwiches and cookies .

Besides all this , the noise from the neighbors with radios destroyed the peacefulness of the occasion . Before long , the sand from the running and the wind covered the blankets and the food . Moreover , the broiling sun heated the soda and the sand . That day , the ocean water had a temperature of only 62 degrees .

Did the parents have any hope for enjoyment ? They just collected everything and everyone . They headed for home .

Practice L: Using the Nominative Case in Sentences of Your Own

[From text, page 267]

Directions: WRITE **THREE** SENTENCES OF YOUR OWN in each of which you **USE *I, HE, SHE, WE, THEY***, and/or ***WHO*** **CORRECTLY**.

____

____

____

Practice M: Using the Objective Case in Sentences of Your Own

[From text, page 267]

Directions: WRITE **FIVE** SENTENCES OF YOUR OWN in each of which you **USE *ME, HER, HIM, US, THEM***, and/or ***WHOM*** **CORRECTLY**.

____

____

____

____

____

PARAGRAPH AND ESSAY SUPPLEMENT

ESSAYS

GOAL IN THIS MINI-CHAPTER
To practice writing essays that include paragraphs developed by definition/clarification, by comparison, and by listing (of some other kind).

ESSAY:
An ESSAY is a collection of paragraphs whose purpose is to tell the reader the writer's views about some (narrowed) topic of interest to both. The core—or BODY—of an essay is the paragraph or paragraphs that treat the angles or categories of particular interest to the writer or the reader. An essay also includes a TITLE (to suggest the content or catch the reader's interest), an INTRODUCTION (to prepare the reader for what is coming), and a CONCLUSION (to draw a lesson from the discussion or simply to bring the writing to a close).

PRACTICE N: PLANNING AN ESSAY WITH PARAGRAPHS DEVELOPED BY DEFINITION/CLARIFICATION, BY COMPARISON, AND BY LISTING

DIRECTIONS: Prepare an essay on a topic that is important to you and that would be of interest to your reader. Choose a specific subject area in which your subject matter needs a definition—that is, a clarification—and you can find a comparison or contrast that will highlight the importance of your message. The third paragraph can contain a listing of advantages, disadvantages, tips, misconceptions, or of anything else that would make your case stronger or clearer. Develop a topic from any of these subject areas or from any other of your own choosing: money, camping, biking, exercising, dieting, studying, sports, some game, friendship, and so forth. First state your three topic ideas (representing the three types of paragraphs) as the "points to be discussed." Then list the supporting points. Finally, write out the gist of what you will say in your introductory and concluding paragraphs. Give some thought to what a good title might be too. Imitate the example outline supplied below.

Example Outline

USING ABBREVIATIONS TO RECORD THE MIND OF A TEACHER

INTRODUCTION: TO KNOW ASSIGNMENTS, TO KNOW WHAT'S MOST IMPORTANT IN A COURSE, AND TO KEEP ALERT

DEFINITION OF ABBREVIATIONS:
- *Use of symbols*
- *No periods*
- *Standard abbreviations*
- *Own abbreviations*
- *Paraphrasing*
- *Omission of unnecessary words like articles*

ADVANTAGES OVER FULL-WORD WORDING
- *More content*
- *Longer-lasting pen/pencil*
- *Less missed altogether*
- *Self-confidence in course*
- *Priceless insights into what teacher feels is most important in course, especially for tests*

TIPS FOR WRITING ABBREVIATIONS FASTER
- *Know and use standard ones.*
- *Know & use symbols.*
- *Use paraphrasing.*
- *Invent own for longer words:*
  - *1st syllable & ending;*
  - *1st two syllables;*
  - *Just consonants (or after 1st syllable).*
- *Invent own for shorter words—but with great care.*
- *Use phonetic spelling for some shorter words.*
- *Leave periods out.*

CONCLUSION: CAUSES CONTINUAL ALERTNESS, ASSURES KNOWING DETAILS OF AN ASSIGNMENT, ASSURES KNOWING THE RELATIVE IMPORTANCE OF CLASS AND TEXTBOOK CONTENT

Practice P: WRITING AN ESSAY WITH PARAGRAPHS DEVELOPED BY DEFINITION/CLARIFICATION, BY COMPARISON, AND BY LISTING

DIRECTIONS: Write an essay based on the outline you prepared for Practice N. Make sure that you use as much repetition and echoing as the subject matter requires. Also be consistent in your use of pronoun reference and tenses. Moreover, add signpost wording wherever possible as a courtesy to your readers. Imitate the example essay supplied below.

Example Paragraph

USING ABBREVIATIONS TO RECORD THE MIND OF A TEACHER

THOUGH IT TAKES PRACTICE TO BECOME GOOD ENOUGH, THERE IS NO SURER WAY OF CAPTURING THE EXACT MIND OF YOUR TEACHER THAN USING ABBREVIATIONS TO MISS NOTHING OF WHAT HE OR SHE SAYS.

YOU MUST UNDERSTAND THAT THE EXPRESSION "USING ABBREVIATIONS" HAS AN UNUSUALLY BROAD MEANING IN THIS DISCUSSION. *I do not mean that you should use just standard abbreviations that you can memorize. Rather, I am referring to any short cut—including such abbreviations—for capturing either the exact wording of your teacher or the closest you can, humanly speaking, come to that. The "abbreviations" that I recommend include symbols and substitute wording (that also can be abbreviated) and omission of the period (that can slow you down); the creation of your own abbreviations that may be of your own deliberate devising for all-purpose use or that are devised by you to meet the vocabulary requirements for a particular course; and abbreviations that you create "on the fly," so to speak, because you do not have time to try to recall some faintly remembered abbreviation.*

THERE ARE CLEAR-CUT ADVANTAGES FOR YOUR USING SUCH "ABBREVIATIONS" OVER YOUR TRYING TO WRITE OUT ALL THE LETTERS OF THE WORDS THAT YOUR TEACHER IS USING. *First, using such abbreviations is the only way to capture on paper everything that your teacher says; in contrast, writing out every word is, practically speaking, impossible. Second, using such abbreviations guarantees—if you must miss something because the teacher is racing—that you miss much less of what is said; in contrast, writing out whole words would cause you to write down too few words to even be meaningful and, probably, to miss even understanding all that the teacher is saying. Finally, using abbreviations gives you confidence that most, if not all, of what the teacher has said is part of your class notes; on the contrary, those who miss whole chunks of what a teacher has said must have worrisome and gnawing misgivings at the time of quizzes and tests.*

HERE ARE SOME TIPS FOR GETTING STARTED USING ABBREVIATIONS SO YOU TOO WILL MISS NOTHING (OR VIRTUALLY NOTHING) OF WHAT A TEACHER SAYS ONCE YOU HAVE PRACTICED USING THEM ENOUGH. *For starters, you should know and use as many of the standard abbreviations as you can find (see your dictionary or a friend's) and that might turn up in a class (for example, the abbreviation for "government" would be "govt").*

In addition, you must look for symbols that can replace words and/or expressions—and in a fraction of the time (for example, ≠ stands for "does not equal" or "is not the same as"). Next, you must practice using beginning letters of long words, often in combination with an ending letter—for example, you would abbreviate "economics" with "econ$^{\underline{s}}$" and "economically" with "econ$^{\underline{ly}}$" (notice how the raised "s" and "ly"—with or without an underline—is a helpful way to indicate an important ending). Another tip or short cut is to form your abbreviations by omitting all the vowels ("a," "e," "i," "o," "u") except for the first one—for example "practically" would become "practcly." Finally, begin making a list of self-created abbreviations (that you must then memorize) of those words that you find yourself using again and again but that take unnecessarily long to write out (for example, you might write "there" as "thr" and "because" as "bec"). However, be careful how you choose an abbreviation for shorter words because we have so many words that can begin and end with the same consonant—for example, "bt" could stand for "bait," "beat," "bite," "boat," "bat," "bit," "but," "bet," "bout," or "boot."

IN CONCLUSION, THESE STRATEGIES FOR USING ABBREVIATIONS PLACE THE OPPORTUNITY IN YOUR OWN HANDS TO KEEP COMPLETE RECORDS OF WHAT EACH TEACHER SAYS. BY MEANS OF THEM, YOU CAN KNOW THE DETAILS OF ASSIGNMENTS AND THE EXTENT OF THE IMPORTANCE IN YOUR TEACHERS' MINDS NOT ONLY OF EVERYTHING SAID IN CLASS BUT ALSO OF THE DIFFERENT SECTIONS OF YOUR TEXTS. LEARN THEM WELL, AND PROFIT FROM THEM ALL YOUR LIFE.

Practice Q: WRITING ANOTHER ESSAY WITH PARAGRAPHS DEVELOPED BY DEFINITION/CLARIFICATION AND BY COMPARISON

DIRECTIONS: Follow the directions of Practices N and P, but write your essay on a different topic.

Chapter 15

Adjectives

Practice A: DETERMINING THE QUESTION ANSWERED BY AN ADJECTIVE

[From text, page 255]

Directions: The adjectives (IN LARGER LETTERING) in each of these sentences answer one of these four questions—***WHICH, WHOSE, HOW MANY/MUCH,*** or ***WHAT KIND OF*** about the noun right after it. IN THE BLANK SPACE TO THE RIGHT OF EACH SENTENCE, WRITE OUT THE QUESTION THAT ITS ADJECTIVE ANSWERS. Imitate the example.

Example: **LITTLE** proof is available. __**HOW MUCH**__

1. **THOROUGH** answers deserve praise. ____________________
2. An **EXPERT'S** opinion has great weight. ____________________
3. **CLOUDLESS** days bring delight to many. ____________________
4. Fires destroyed **COUNTLESS** acres. ____________________
5. Einstein's theories raised **SOME** questions too. ____________________
6. All have received **THEIR** grades. ____________________
7. Some **OAK** trees keep their leaves longest. ____________________
8. **THESE** chapters require concentration. ____________________
9. **FEW** decisions remain to be made. ____________________
10. Half-hearted effort achieves **LITTLE** good. ____________________

Practice B: FINDING ADJECTIVES INSIDE NOUN CLUSTERS

[From text, page 276]

Directions: For each of these noun clusters, WRITE **ADJ** OVER ALL ADJECTIVES. The nouns and pronouns have been labeled for you. Imitate the example.

Examples:

(ADV)	ADJ	ADJ	N
somewhat	older	brick	houses

PRN	ADJ
anything	unusual

1. few genuine paintings (N: paintings)
2. something spectacular (PRN: something)
3. many quite unusual sunsets (N: sunsets)
4. rather noisy old car (N: car)
5. thick, rich, fattening cream (N: cream)
6. someone important (PRN: someone)
7. everything else (PRN: everything)
8. this fairly simple mathematical problem (N: problem)
9. nothing worthwhile (PRN: nothing)
10. somewhat outdated songs (N: songs)

Practice C: Labeling of Prepositional Phrases That Do the Job of an Adjective

[From text, page 277]

Directions: For these expressions, **first** LABEL ANY PREPOSITIONS; **second,** LABEL ANY OBJECT OF PREPOSITION; **third,** LABEL **ALL ADJECTIVES, INCLUDING ANY PREPOSITIONAL PHRASE THAT DOES THE JOB OF AN ADJECTIVE**. The chief nouns and pronouns have been labeled for you. Imitate the example.

OP
(ADV) N ADJ OP
ADJ N
Example: in areas of excessive flooding

N N
1. longer, warmer days of spring

PRN N
2. no one with old sneakers

N N
3. on top of her world

N N
4. with little chance of failure

N N
5. every sign of eventual success

N N
6. somewhat frequent calls from home

N
7. some sturdy, wooden, oaken chairs

N
8. much rather sophisticated machin-ery

Practice D: Identifying Articles

[From text, page 278]

Directions: For these expressions, **first** LABEL EVERY PREPOSITION; **second,** LABEL EVERY OBJECT OF PREPOSITION; **third,** LABEL ALL **ARTICLES**; **fourth,** LABEL ALL ADJECTIVES, INCLUDING ALL PREPOSITIONAL PHRASES THAT DO THE JOB OF AN ADJECTIVE. The chief nouns and pronouns have been labeled for you. Imitate the example.

OP
ART N ADJ ART N
Example: the beginning of the story

N N
1. for the rest of the day

N
2. a rather large, lazy snowflake

N N
3. an answer to the question

N N
4. in the wake of a fast boat

N N
5. the amazing light of a full moon

N N
6. on a drawer of the desk

N N
7. an invitation from a friend

N N
8. an increase of humid weather

Practice E: Carrying out Tests 1–8, through Step 1A—Labeling Proper Nouns

[From text, page 284]

Directions: For these sentences, CARRY OUT TESTS 1–8, and **place an N—AND overhead brace as necessary—over all PROPER NOUNS.** Imitate the example.

[is] Ⓢ N MS OP N

Example: ^ The Indian Ocean is in the Southern Hemisphere.

1. General Motors bought Hughes Aircraft Corporation at considerable cost.

2. The St. Lawrence River separates the United States from Canada.

3. Lee Iacocca has done wonders for Chrysler Motors Corporation.

4. The Adirondack Mountain Range in New York State has a spectacular beauty.

5. When lightning struck the home of the Browns, they moved to Jersey City.

6. The maple syrup from Vermont reaches homes in Pennsylvania.

Practice F: LABELING KEYWORD NOUNS

[From text, page 285]

Directions: For these expressions, USE THE THE TEST TO FIND ANY **NOUN**. Then label the noun with an **N.**

Examples: the rather tall sapling (N over *sapling*)

someone special [You cannot say ~~*the someone*~~; *someone* is a pronoun, not a noun.]

1. many huge rocks
2. the bright, clear day
3. everything possible
4. the numerous small twigs
5. several rather pretty plants
6. the fruit provided
7. anything unusual
8. countless young, light green leaves

Practice G: LABELING KEYWORD NOUNS

[From text, page 286]

Directions: For these expressions, USE THE THE TEST TO FIND ANY **NOUN**. Then label the noun with an **N.**

Example: an educated guess (N over *guess*) [When you say *the educated*, you mean *educated* in the sense of "skilled in letters," not in the sense here of "partly informed."]

1. the strenuous exercise
2. the tickets available
3. a rather old, gnarled tree
4. everyone involved
5. something special
6. the opening song
7. a strong, manly handshake
8. some rather smart decisions

Practice H: LABELING KEYWORD NOUNS

[From text, page 286]

Directions: For these expressions, LABEL ALL **NOUNS, ADJECTIVES,** AND **ARTICLES**. Imitate the example.

	ADJ	ADJ	ADJ	N
Example:	this	year's	barbershop	quartet

1. a handy laundry chute

2. a red tape dispenser

3. several start-up options

4. a small paper cup

5. the passengers aboard

6. an easy assignment

7. a sample piece

8. decorative cookie cutters

Practice J: CARRYING OUT TESTS 1–8, THROUGH STEP 1—LABELING KEYWORDS

[From text, page 286]

Directions: For these sentences, CARRY OUT TESTS 1–8, THROUGH LABELING ALL **KEYWORD NOUNS. Also label articles and adjectives—including any prepositional phrase that does the job of an adjective.** Imitate the example.

Example:

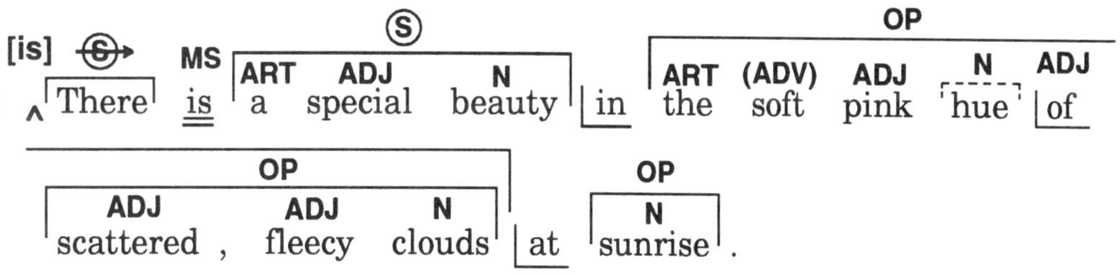

1. In what month does the nighttime temperature reach thirty-two degrees ?

2. [If a flock of geese ever settled in a nearby field], you would wonder at their raucous [*annoyingly harsh*] noisiness .

3. [Because an indoors dog gains significant weight in winter], one can carry it for its bath with far less ease .

4. Shouldn't an informed student judge [that part-time work interferes with his more important job of success at school work] ?
(INT printed above "that")

Practice K: Carrying out Tests 1–8, through Step 2—Labeling Keyword Pronouns

[From text, page 287]

Directions: For these sentences, CARRY OUT TESTS 1–8, THROUGH LABELING **KEYWORD PRONOUNS. Also label articles and adjectives —including any prepositional phrase that does the job of an adjective.** Imitate the example.

[does] Ⓢ MS [does require] OV INT S [do give] OV
PRN ADJ PRN ADJ

Example: ^Something worthwhile ^requires [that you ^give undivided

N OP PRN

attention to it .]

Instant House

Why has our rural road had more traffic recently ? Someone new is building his house in the field by our house . At a hearing concerning [a preposition] the subdivision of the land , we met one of the family members .

INT

He said [that everything was on schedule] . If nothing unexpected occurred, everyone would be moving into [preposition] the house by January first . They had only started the building in early October .

Practice L: CARRYING OUT TESTS 1–8

[From text, page 288]

Directions: For these sentences, CARRY OUT ALL THE STEPS FOR TESTS 1–8.

A Horse in Need

An asthmatic horse must be fed separately from any other horses .

Otherwise , the companion horses will eat all her food [before she can have

her fill] . What [pronoun] else but [preposition] a slow death would such truly

heartless treatment of a horse cause ? [If you were an owner [predicate noun]

of such a horse] , would you permit that kind of almost unbelievable cruelty?

Practice M: CARRYING OUT TESTS 1–8

[From text, page 288]

Directions: For these sentences, CARRY OUT ALL THE STEPS FOR TESTS 1–8.

Everything in Its Place

Sometimes disorderliness causes problems for a person . This has happened to a fairly good friend of mine .

He has a rather spacious garage [where he places his many tools] . [When he finishes some project] , does he always place his tools [where they belong] ? This does not happen.

[Because his favorite tools cannot now be found so easily] , his jobs require much more time . What simple task will he abandon next [because he cannot find some sorely needed tool] ?

Practice N: USING THE ARTICLE A CORRECTLY

[From text, page 289]

Directions: USE THE ARTICLE ***A*** CORRECTLY BEFORE SIX WORDS OF YOUR OWN CHOOSING.

______________________ ______________________

______________________ ______________________

______________________ ______________________

Practice P: USING THE ARTICLE AN CORRECTLY

[From text, page 289]

Directions: USE THE ARTICLE ***AN*** CORRECTLY BEFORE SIX WORDS OF YOUR OWN CHOOSING.

______________________ ______________________

______________________ ______________________

______________________ ______________________

Practice Q: USING ITS CORRECTLY

[From text, page 289]

Directions: WRITE THREE SENTENCES OF YOUR OWN USING ***ITS*** CORRECTLY.

____

____

____

Practice R: Using *Their, They're,* and *There* Correctly

[From text, page 290]

Directions: Write nine sentences of your own. Write **THREE using *THEIR* as an adjective correctly; THREE using *THEY'RE* correctly; and THREE using *THERE* correctly.** Please place your sentences where the labels request them.

[THEIR] ______________________________

____

____

[THEY'RE] ______________________________

____

____

[THERE] ______________________________

____

____

Practice S: Using the Apostrophe or Apostrophe + *S* for the Possessive Form of Nouns Correctly

[From text, page 291]

Directions: Write six sentences of your own. **Write THREE using just an apostrophe (') and THREE using an APOSTROPHE + S ('S) correctly.** Please place your sentences where the labels request them.

['] ______________________________

____

____

['S] ______________________________

____

____

Practice T: USING THE *ER* ENDING FOR ADJECTIVES CORRECTLY

[From text, page 292]

Directions: WRITE THREE SENTENCES OF YOUR OWN. In each, **use correctly an ADJECTIVE WITH AN *ER* ENDING.**

Practice U: USING THE *EST* ENDING FOR AN ADJECTIVE CORRECTLY

[From text, page 292]

Directions: WRITE THREE SENTENCES OF YOUR OWN. In each, **use correctly an ADJECTIVE WITH AN *EST* ENDING.**

Practice V: WRITING SENTENCES THAT USE ONLY ONE COMPARATIVE FORM

[From text, page 293]

Directions: WRITE FIVE SENTENCES OF YOUR OWN, and **use a CORRECT COMPARISON IN EACH.**

Paragraph and Essay Supplement

Essays Again

> **Goal in This Mini-Chapter**
>
> **To practice writing essays that include paragraphs by anecdote, by comparison, and by listing (of some other kind).**

Practice W: Planning an Essay with Paragraphs Developed by Anecdote, by Comparison, and by Listing

Directions: Prepare an essay on a topic that is important to you and that would be of interest to your reader. Choose a specific subject area in which you can find an anecdote or story to support or "prove" your point and a comparison or contrast that will highlight the importance of your message. The third paragraph can contain a listing of advantages, disadvantages, tips, misconceptions, or of anything else that would make your case stronger or clearer. Develop a topic from any of these subject areas or from any other of your own choosing: food, clothing, water, apartment living, housing, shopping, alcohol, drugs, and so forth. First state your three topic ideas (representing the three types of paragraphs) as the "points to be discussed." Then list the supporting points. Finally, write out the gist of what you will say in your introductory and concluding paragraphs. Give some thought to what a good title might be too. Imitate the type of outline supplied as an example in chapter 14.

Practice X: Writing an Essay with Paragraphs Developed by Anecdote, by Comparison, and by Listing

Directions: Write an essay based on the outline you prepared for Practice W. Make sure that you use as much repetition and echoing as the subject matter requires. Also be consistent in your use of pronoun reference and tenses. Moreover, add signpost wording wherever possible as a courtesy to your readers. Imitate the type of essay supplied as an example in chapter 14.

Practice Y: Writing a Second Essay with Paragraphs Developed by Anecdote, by Comparison, and by Listing

Directions: Follow the directions of Practice W, but write your essay on a different topic.

Chapter 16

Adverbs

Practice A: DETERMINING THE QUESTION ANSWERED BY AN ADVERB

[From text, page 300]

Directions: FILL THE BLANK SPACE AFTER EACH OF THESE SENTENCES WITH THE QUESTION THAT ITS ADVERB (IN CAPITALIZED AND DARKER LETTERING) ANSWERS. Choose among the questions ***HOW, HOW OFTEN, WHEN, WHERE, WHY,*** and ***UNDER WHAT CIRCUMSTANCES***. Imitate the example.

Example: The package has **NOT** arrived. **UNDER WHAT CIRCUMSTANCES**

1. The sun rose **SLOWLY.** ____________________
2. Rosemary said nothing **DELIBERATELY.** ____________________
3. The workers started **PROMPTLY.** ____________________
4. Owls are **SELDOM** seen in the day. ____________________
5. The dog walked **HOME.** ____________________
6. The overtired student studied **FRUITLESSLY**. ____________________
7. **GRADUALLY** new insights developed. ____________________
8. Students should **NEVER** try for less than an "A." ____________________
9. We have a **RATHER** ill cat. ____________________
10. **EVENINGS** Doug has a second job. ____________________
11. This is **UNQUESTIONABLY** right. ____________________
12. We should not give **SO** sparingly. ____________________

Practice B: FINDING ADVERBS THAT MODIFY VERBS OR VERBS PLUS THEIR COMPANION WORDING

[From text, page 303]

Directions: For the sentences in this passage, CARRY OUT TESTS 1–8. **In addition, FIND AND LABEL ALL ADVERBS.** Imitate the example.

Example: FAV ⟨Silently⟩, ^[did] [ART the N cat] (S) ^[did look] ~~looked~~ ADV about ADV everywhere .

Life-Threatening Dangers

An inexperienced homeowner can easily think [INT that he has adequate lumberjack skills]. He somehow thinks [INT that leaning trees will always fall forward [if he cuts them right]]. However , a tree's greatest weight might just lie on an unanticipated side somehow . Similarly , a gust of wind has occasionally blown a tree down in unexpected directions too . Besides , some ornery trees simply choose their own resting place. Indeed , a homeowner must expect an unforeseeable accident [if he performs such dangerous tasks] .

Practice C: Labeling Adverbs and Adverbial Prepositional Phrases

[From text, page 303]

Directions: For the sentences in this passage, CARRY OUR TESTS 1–8. **In addition, find and label all adverbs AND PREPOSITIONAL PHRASES THAT DO THE JOB OF AN ADVERB.** Imitate the example.

Example:

FAV OP: ⟨With [ADJ some N difficulty]⟩, [did] Ⓢ [ART the N boys] MS [did pitch] pitched OV [ADJ their N tent]

ADV at OP [ART the N top ADJ of OP [ART the N mountain]] ADV by OP [N nightfall].

Hurricanes

[If you have ever experienced a hurricane] , you have experienced something terrifying . [When a friend of mine was in the Philippines once] , the "eye" of the hurricane passed overhead [where he was then staying] . Obviously , everyone took cover for the duration of the storm . The wind struck the buildings with the force of a ramrod . Houses shook to their foundations . Many native houses just collapsed like [preposition] cardboard . Everywhere pieces of tin from roofs were sailing by people . There was no safe place nearby for homeless people. How many unfortunate Filipinos must have been injured ?

Practice D: Labeling Adverbs That Modify an Adjective or Another Adverb

[From text, page 306]

Directions: For these expressions, CARRY OUT ALL TESTS POSSIBLE. **In addition, LABEL AS ADVERBS THOSE WORDS THAT COME BEFORE AN ADJECTIVE OR ADVERB—OR BEFORE A PREPOSITIONAL PHRASE DOING THE JOB OF AN ADJECTIVE OR ADVERB—AND ANSWER *HOW* WHEN ASKED THERE.** Imitate the example.

Examples:

	ADV	ADJ	N		
	somewhat	tired	worker		
[did sleep]	ADV	ADV			
^ slept	very	late			
[did place]	OV: ADJ	N	ADV	ADV	OP
^ placed	his	coat	right	by	mine

1. talks quite quickly
2. extremely brisk breeze
3. arrived just in time
4. walked that far
5. somewhat dirty sneakers
6. partially cleaned windshield
7. worked well past [preposition] midnight
8. overly ambitious plans

Practice E: CARRYING OUT ALL THE TESTS

[From text, page 307]

Directions: For this passage, CARRY OUT TESTS 1–9 IN FULL.

Driving

My mother does not much like driving for a pastime . She will rarely leave the house just for a drive . [When everyone is home on weekends now] , she rather suddenly finds herself always in the car . For instance , she brought an overnight guest of my sister home today . Then she brought another sister of mine to a baby-sitting job . Right now she is returning from a trip to town with still another overnight guest . In the light of this , what might tomorrow bring ? [If tomorrow brings an eagerly sought weekday] , it can only bring peaceful rest to an overly wearied human being .

Practice F: USING THE ADVERB *TOO* CORRECTLY

[From text, page 308]

Directions: WRITE FOUR SENTENCES OF YOUR OWN in which you USE THE ADVERB ***TOO*** CORRECTLY. Use the first two lines to write two sentences where it has the meaning *also*. Use the next two lines to write two sentences where it has the meaning *excessively*.

[***TOO***=*also*] ____

____

[***TOO***=*excessively*] ____

____

Practice G: WRITING SENTENCES USING ADVERBS CORRECTLY

[From text, page 309]

Directions: WRITE **ONE** SENTENCE FOR EACH OF THESE **THREE** **ADVERBS**—***FAITHFULLY, GRADUALLY,*** **and** ***PERFECTLY***. Be sure to use each adverb correctly.

____

____

____

Practice H: WRITING SENTENCES USING ADJECTIVES CORRECTLY

[From text, page 309]

Directions: WRITE **ONE** SENTENCE FOR EACH OF THESE **THREE** **ADJECTIVES**—***FAITHFUL, GRADUAL,*** **and** ***PERFECT***. Be sure to use each adjective correctly.

____

____

____

PARAGRAPH AND ESSAY SUPPLEMENT

PROOF

GOALS IN THIS MINI-CHAPTER

To practice writing paragraphs developed by proof from authority and statistics and an essay that includes paragraphs of proof by authority, statistics, and anecdote.

PARAGRAPH OF PROOF BY AUTHORITY

A paragraph that seeks to PROVE some point relative to one's topic by quoting or paraphrasing the words of an AUTHORITY (that is, an expert in a field) who has acceptable credentials and who is unbiased.

Practice J: PLANNING A PARAGRAPH DEVELOPED BY PROOF FROM AUTHORITY

DIRECTIONS: Plan a paragraph in which you prove some point related to your topic by quoting the words of an authority—a person whom you prove, as best you can, to be an "authority." You can find excellent source material in the *Reader's Digest,* the newsmagazines *Time, Newsweek,* and *U.S. News & World Report* and in articles in newspapers. Write out the point that the words of the authority are to prove as the "point under discussion." Then jot down—in outline format—all the information you need to add to complete your proof—namely: the words to be quoted or paraphrased, the reputation of the authority, the freedom of the authority from bias (with respect to your point) if possible, and the source of your information. Imitate the example outline supplied below.

Example Outline

A PROGRAM OF STRENUOUS EXERCISE CAUSES MENTAL ALERTNESS

Dr. Morehouse states:
"It dispels late-day drag . . .";
"You can stay up late when you have to . . .";
"You can work an occasional eighteen-hour day and not need a week to recover."

Trustworthiness of Dr. Morehouse:
Author of book Total Fitness in 30 Minutes a Week
Expert in physiology of exercise
Selected by the National Academy of Science to devise the means of keeping our astronauts fit in space—on both the trip to the moon and in the Skylab program
Practices what he preaches

Practice K: WRITING A PARAGRAPH DEVELOPED BY PROOF FROM AUTHORITY

DIRECTIONS: Write a paragraph based on the outline you prepared for Practice J. Indicate the source of your information (including page numbers), and choose the correct punctuation marks for identifying titles—use italics/underlining for labeling major titles (those of books, magazines, and newspapers) and quotation marks for labeling lesser titles (articles, chapters, and TV programs). Also be sure to place your closing quotation marks AFTER any period or comma. Make sure, too, that you use as much repetition and echoing as the subject matter requires. Finally, be consistent in your use of pronoun reference and tenses. Imitate the example paragraph supplied below.

Example Paragraph

A PROGRAM THAT INCLUDES STRENUOUS PHYSICAL EXERCISE CAUSES US TO BE MORE ALERT MENTALLY. *In his recent book Total Fitness in 30 Minutes a Week (N.Y.: Simon and Schuster, 1975, 31), Dr. Laurence Morehouse made this claim for his fitness program. He stated: "It dispels late-day drag . . . . You can stay up late when you have to. You can work an occasional eighteen-hour day and not need a week to recover." Morehouse, by the way, is the expert in the physiology of exercise who was selected by the National Academy of Science to develop the means to keep astronauts fit both while on the moon and in the Skylab program. In 1975, his other book The Physiology of Exercise was the standard text for colleges and universities throughout the world.*

PARAGRAPH OF PROOF BY STATISTICS

A paragraph that uses STATISTICS or DATA from a study—that was designed to prove the point at hand and was correctly conducted—as proof of some point relative to one's topic. This kind of proof is especially effective when combined with proof by anecdote and/or by authority for use in both informative and persuasive essays.

Practice L: PLANNING A PARAGRAPH DEVELOPED BY PROOF FROM STATISTICS

DIRECTIONS: Plan a paragraph in which you prove some point related to your topic by referring to valid and reliable statistical data. Such data are valid if the purpose of the study or research was to prove the point that you are making and if it used methods that were suitable for the task. The data are reliable if they can be or have been duplicated—that is, if they were proven true at least a second time—and if alternative explanations of the results have been proven to be unacceptable. Use the same type of source material that you did for Practice J. Write out the point that your statistics or data prove as your "point under discussion." Then jot down—in outline format—all the information you need to add to complete your proof—namely: how the study was designed to prove the very point that you are making; the circumstances of the study, especially as they relate to the care and thoroughness with which the study was conducted; the source of your information; and the lack of bias of the researchers (to the extent this information may be available). Imitate the example outline supplied below.

Example Outline

ONE QUARTER OF AMERICANS RISK PREMATURE DEATH AND UNNECESSARY ILL HEALTH:

26% are cigarette smokers.
Cigarette smoke kills 418,000 in U.S. yearly.
It is the leading cause of preventable death.
Other effects: sickness, loss of work, misery.
Source: Time magazine article.

Practice M: WRITING A PARAGRAPH DEVELOPED BY PROOF FROM STATISTICS

DIRECTIONS: Write a paragraph based on the outline you prepared for Practice L. Indicate the source of your information (including page numbers), and choose the correct punctuation marks for identifying titles—use italics/underlining for labeling major titles (those of books, magazines, and newspapers) and quotation marks for labeling lesser titles (articles, chapters, and TV programs). Also be sure to place your closing quotation marks AFTER any period or comma. Make sure, too, that you use as much repetition and echoing as the subject matter requires. Finally, be consistent in your use of pronoun reference and tenses. Imitate the example paragraph supplied below.

Example Paragraph

TWENTY-SIX PERCENT OF AMERICANS PLAY RUSSIAN ROULETTE WITH THEIR HEALTH—AND THEIR WALLET. *This is because they smoke cigarettes, and cigarette smoke* ***kills*** *418,000 Americans—close to half a million—every year, according to the Centers for Disease Control and Prevention. In fact, cigarette smoking is the leading cause of preventable death in our country today. It goes without saying that it is also the cause of untold and prolonged illness and suffering and of loss of work—and salary. The above percentage and number of deaths were reported in the carefully researched Time cover-story article "The Butt Stops Here" (April 18, 1994, page 61).*

Practice N: WRITING AN ESSAY THAT IS DEVELOPED BY PARAGRAPHS OF PROOF FROM AUTHORITY, STATISTICS, AND AN ANECDOTE

DIRECTIONS: Plan and write an essay that proves something important to know. In both your outline and your essay, include the following: a title, an introduction, a paragraph of proof based on authority, a paragraph of proof based on statistical data, a paragraph of proof based on an anecdote, and a conclusion. Make sure that each of your paragraphs of proof STARTS WITH A TOPIC SENTENCE THAT IS RELATED TO YOUR ESSAY (your proof, of course, must prove the statement in your topic sentence). Use the same type of source materials that you did for Practices J and L above. Note that most *Reader's Digest* articles include an anecdote that you can adapt for your own use. Indicate the source of your information, and—as in Practices J and K above—use quotation marks and underlining correctly.

Chapter 17

Introduction to Dependent Clauses

Practice A: CARRYING OUT ALL TESTS

See text, page 318.

Directions: First, CARRY OUT TESTS 1–7 (THROUGH THE NOUN-JOB TESTS). Second, **find and label all DEPENDENT CLAUSES AND THEIR INTRODUCERS**. Third, **carry out the Adjective Test and Adverb Test**. Imitate the example.

Example:

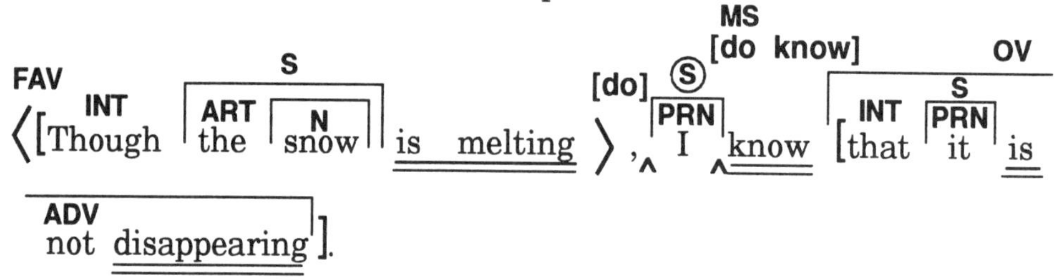

1. If you take a picture, you should release the shutter only when everyone is smiling.

2. If you shovel snow in time, you avoid unnecessary trouble later.

3. When someone jogs for exercise, he/she should wear shoes with cushioned soles.

4. Cooks know that the right length of time for cooking prevents disaster.

5. When the sun sets later, everyone knows that summertime is approaching.

6. Though a friend has called on the phone , your conversation could interfere with your studying if you talk too long.

Practice B: CARRYING OUT ALL TESTS AND LABELING NOUN CLAUSES

See text, page 321.

Directions: First, CARRY OUT TESTS 1–7 (THROUGH THE NOUN-JOB TESTS). Second, **find and label all DEPENDENT CLAUSES AND THEIR INTRODUCERS**. Third, **carry out the Adjective and Adverb Tests**. Imitate the example.

OV
[could] Ⓢ PRN MS ADV OV ADJ (INT) N

Example: ^ We could seldom guess [which questions

S
ART N
the teacher would ask].

1. He could not decide whom he should give the award to .

2. No one heard what the President had said .

3. How much aid we should give to the poor can not be easily decided .

4. Could you learn where this word originated ?

5. Whose art work would get first prize was now being judged .

6. Why do you ask what name you should give to the first word of a clause ?

Practice C: CARRYING OUT ALL TESTS AND LABELING NOUN CLAUSES AND ADVERB CLAUSES

See text, page 321.

Directions: First, CARRY OUT TESTS 1–7 (THROUGH THE NOUN-JOB TESTS). Second, **find and label all DEPENDENT CLAUSES AND THEIR INTRODUCERS**. Third, **carry out the Adjective and Adverb Tests**.

Party Time

When my mother said that I could have some friends over for my birthday , neither of us suspected that the final number would come to sixteen . When the day finally arrived , all of us met in town . After we played baseball for two hours , we drove to our house for some pizza . Then my two brothers took us to a campsite where we played games until we closed our eyes at three in the morning .

Do you think that my friends will ever forget that occasion ?

Practice D: Carrying out All Tests and Labeling Adjective Clauses

See text, page 323.

Directions: First, CARRY OUT TESTS 1–7 (THROUGH THE NOUN-JOB TESTS). Second, **find and label all DEPENDENT CLAUSES AND THEIR INTRODUCERS**. Third, **carry out the Adjective and Adverb Tests**. Imitate the example.

Ⓢ

[is] ART N ADJ S (INT) PRN OV ART N MS ADV OP ART N

Example: ^ The wind [which is driving the snow] is from the south .

1. A friend who fishes in Idaho catches unusually big fish .

2. The magazines to which I am attracted have articles on computers .

3. The season which I most look forward to has now arrived .

4. The people at whose house Ed has stayed have moved to Arizona .

5. The guest arrived at the time when everyone was studying for exams .

6. They gave no reason why they could not provide a lane for bicyclists .

Practice E: CARRYING OUT ALL TESTS

See text, page 323.

Directions: First, CARRY OUT TESTS 1–7 (THROUGH THE NOUN-JOB TESTS). Second, **find and label all DEPENDENT CLAUSES AND THEIR INTRODUCERS**. Third, **carry out the Adjective and Adverb Tests**.

Company

Since Thanksgiving vacation came late somehow , we had extra company at our house . While we usually have one guest who might stay longer , we now had two guests . They stayed from Monday until the weekend came . Although my father needed time for a backlog of paper correcting , he could not find enough time . If he ever has these guests again , he will say that they must not stay so long . Otherwise , they can come after the school session has ended . Until this semester passes , he will be under [preposition] great pressure because good sense did not win out .

Practice F: CARRYING OUT ALL THE TESTS

See text, page 324.

Directions: CARRY OUT ALL THE TESTS (**AND** STEPS) TO FOLLOW TO SUCCEED—**and in the right order**.

Successful Students

Why wouldn't every student want success in school since so much depends on it ? Students who want success in a class must get grades which excel from the start . Also , success comes to students who have questions for their teachers . Which questions do not improve understanding when students present them with sincerity ? Some students who excel in their studies compete with friends who are also doing well . Haven't students with grades which impress their friends also used flash cards , which assure better remembering ?

Practice G: Carrying out All Tests

See text, page 324.

Directions: Carry out all the Tests (**and** Steps) to Follow to Succeed—**and in the right order**.

Faltering Students

Students who falter in school have often not learned that there are ways in which they can hurt their own learning ability . When you think for a while , you think of students who do not sleep enough . If you think some more , you think of students who assume that last-minute studying best prepares them for some test . After you think again , you think of students who nod in class from the fatigue of late watching of TV .

When will students realize that right living causes students who do right learning ?

PARAGRAPH AND ESSAY SUPPLEMENT

PERSUASION

GOAL IN THIS MINI-CHAPTER

To practice writing persuasive essays that include paragraphs that counter objections; list steps; and offer proof from paragraphs by anecdote, authority, and/or statistics.

THE PARAGRAPH THAT COUNTERS OBJECTIONS

A paragraph that counters objections is a paragraph that states an OBJECTION (an argument in your readers' minds in opposition to your proposal) and then counters (REFUTES) it by demonstrating its irrelevance or inaccuracy. You must mention—and then oppose with the strongest arguments you can—all the chief objections of your readers in any essay whose purpose is to effectively persuade the reader to change an attitude or adopt a new course of action.

PRACTICE H: PLANNING A PERSUASIVE ESSAY

DIRECTIONS: Plan a persuasive essay on a topic that you feel strongly about. Use a single source—such as the *Reader's Digest, Time, Newsweek, U.S. News & World Report,* or a newspaper article—if you can. In both your outline and your essay, include the following: a cleverly worded TITLE; an INTRODUCTION that catches a reader's attention; one or two paragraphs that counter OBJECTIONS that your readers might have; at least two paragraphs of PROOF based on anecdote, authority, and/or statistics that are sound and convincing; a paragraph that lists realistic STEPS that your readers should carry out; and a CONCLUSION that will help them see themselves enjoying the benefits of what you propose or suffering the consequences if they do not. Make sure that each of your paragraphs STARTS WITH A TOPIC SENTENCE THAT IS RELATED TO YOUR ESSAY (your proofs, of course, must prove the statements in your topic sentences). Also make your writing as personal as possible by relating your discussion to the lives of the readers, at least by hypothetical situations but also by comparisons and image-filled language as much as possible. As usual, include the gist of what you will say in your introduction and conclusion; and for all other paragraphs, write out the "point to be discussed/proven"—the base for your topic sentences—as the heading. Then add the details that support your statement. Imitate the example outline supplied below.

Example Outline

ONE-TWO-THREE: YOU HAVE SAVED A LIFE

INTRODUCTION: ***IF A PERSON BESIDE YOU IN A SUBWAY, CAFETERIA, OR ELEVATOR WERE TO HAVE A HEART ATTACK AND GO INTO CARDIAC ARREST, COULD YOU PERSONALLY DO MORE THAN JUST WATCH HIM OR HER DIE? YES—YOU CAN, WITHOUT TRAINING, PERFORM CPR (CARDIOPULMONARY RESUSCITATION).***

OBJECTION: ***I COULD INJURE THE PERSON.***
The person could die!

OBJECTION: ***I HAVE NO TRAINING.***
Any help could save the person.

PROOF OF NEED: ***HARM BEGINS AFTER 4 MINUTES.***
In 10 minutes there's brain damage, and ambulances take 10 minutes to arrive.

PROOF OF NEED: ***VERY OFTEN, ONLY ONE WILLING BYSTANDER IS NEEDED.***
60% of people with cardiac arrest do have bystanders near them.

THERE IS A CITY WHERE BYSTANDERS HELP AND MAKE A DIFFERENCE:
In Seattle, 50–60% get help from a bystander and that city has the best record in the country for lives saved.

THE AMERICAN HEART ASSOCIATION RECOMMENDS 3 STEPS:
Lift the chin.
Breathe into the person's mouth until the chest rises, twice.
Press the heel of your hand into person's chest 15 times.
You can get instruction too.

CONCLUSION: ***PICTURE SOMEONE ALIVE AND WELL (AND NOT DEAD) SOLELY BECAUSE OF YOUR WILLINGNESS TO HELP—HOW GRATEFUL THE PERSON MUST BE AND HOW PROUD YOU ARE OF YOURSELF!***

PRACTICE J: WRITING A PERSUASIVE ESSAY

DIRECTIONS: Write an essay based on the outline you prepared for Practice H. Indicate the source of your information, and use quotation marks and underlining correctly. Imitate the example essay supplied below.

Example Essay

ONE-TWO-THREE: YOU HAVE SAVED A LIFE

SUPPOSE A PERSON BESIDE YOU—AT SCHOOL, AT HOME, ON A BUS—SUDDENLY WENT INTO CARDIAC ARREST AND STOPPED BREATHING, COULD THAT PERSON'S LIFE DEPEND ON A FEW SIMPLE STEPS THAT EVEN YOU COULD PERFORM IF ONLY YOU KNEW THEM? *The answer is an unqualified YES. Cardiopulmonary resuscitation or CPR is not a remote, schoolbook science but a few simple acts of human kindness that you too can and should know how to perform.*

YOU MAY OBJECT THAT YOU WOULD ONLY INJURE THE PERSON IF YOU TRIED TO GIVE HELP. *The fact is that inaction on your part will certainly result in either the death of that person or in extensive brain damage because brain damage is a certainty even if an ambulance arrives as quickly as in ten minutes. In fact, the brain begins to die within four minutes after blood circulation stops. By the way, in most cities the typical amount of time it takes for an ambulance to arrive in cases of cardiac arrest is ten long minutes. (All citations here are from Jane E. Brody's "CPR: Now It's Easy" article in the July, 1994, issue of the Reader's Digest, pages 87–90.)*

YOU MUST NOT THINK THAT CPR IS ONLY FOR THOSE TRAINED TO USE IT. *If there is no one at hand who has been trained, "any CPR is better than none," according to Dr. Richard O. Cummins, Director of Emergency Cardiac Care in King County, Washington. "When the choice is a broken rib, bruised lung* ***or loss of life*** *[emphasis added]—the right choice should be obvious," declares Brody. As a matter of fact, doing the chest compressions alone (see below) could possibly save such a person's life because it causes the three-to-four-minute supply of oxygen that is still in the blood to reach the organs that sustain life.*

THE STATISTICS SUGGEST HOW IMPORTANT YOUR HELP IS. *Three out of every five heart attacks that result in cardiac arrest occur in the presence of a bystander who—by applying the three steps listed below—could save that person's life. In addition, two thirds of the deaths from this illness take place before the victims can reach a hospital.*

THE FACT THAT YOU, THE BYSTANDER, CAN MAKE A DIFFERENCE HAS BEEN PROVEN IN SEATTLE. *There, 50–60% of heart-attack victims receive CPR from a bystander. That city has the nation's best record for survival after a witnessed cardiac arrest!*

ACCORDING TO THE AMERICAN HEART ASSOCIATION, THERE ARE THREE STEPS THAT EVEN YOU CAN EASILY PERFORM—PROVIDED YOU HAVE DETERMINED THAT THE PERSON HAS

STOPPED BREATHING AND THAT THE PERSON'S PULSE HAS STOPPED. *FIRST—but AFTER calling or having someone else call for emergency help—open the person's air passageways by lifting the chin up, while the person is on his or her back. SECOND, breathe slowly into the person's mouth until the person's chest rises—TWICE (be sure to keep the nostrils pinched so no air can escape through them). THREE, immediately press down on the person's chest* ***15 times****—to the count of "one-and, two-and, three-and," and so forth: you must position the heel of one hand on the middle of the chest between the nipples and press vertically downwards with your elbows straight (to force the oxygen in the blood to circulate especially to the brain). After four sets of this approximately 11-second routine, you should check the person's breathing and pulse again. Continue these sets of four routines until there are both breathing and a pulse—even after that, a person could unexpectedly stop breathing or lose his/her pulse so keep checking. (If you want to become truly skilled, you can also take a course; simply call 1-800-AHA-USA1 for the nearest location.)*

JUST IMAGINE YOURSELF ABLE TO BRING NORMAL LIFE BACK TO A PERSON—JUST ONE PERSON—THROUGH THESE THREE ACTS OF SIMPLE HUMAN KINDNESS (LIFTING THE CHIN, SHARING YOUR BREATH, AND SHARING THE STRENGTH OF YOUR BACK). *How grateful that person would be! How proud you would be of yourself! Remember—always—the need to lift the chin, share your breath twice, and press down on the person's chest 15 times* ***and*** *to act promptly if opportunity knocks.*

Practice K: WRITING ANOTHER PERSUASIVE ESSAY

DIRECTIONS: Write a persuasive essay on a different topic from the one chosen for Practices H and J, but use exactly the same directions.

Appendix

Rules for Agreement of a Verb with Its Subject

Practice A: Making Verbs Agree with the Keyword in the Subject

[From text, page 327]

Directions: WRITE SIX SENTENCES OF YOUR OWN. For the **first** THREE sentences, use a SINGULAR subject in the **third** person (like *boy*). For the **last** THREE sentences, use a PLURAL subject in the **third** person (like *boys*). Use only the **present tense** or ***was*** or ***were*** or ***has*** or ***have***. Imitate the examples.

Examples: [SINGULAR] A **WILDFLOWER is** often hidden.

[PLURAL] **WILDFLOWERS are** often beautiful.

[SINGULAR] ______________________________

____

____

[PLURAL] ______________________________

____

____

Practice B: WRITING SENTENCES WITH SPACE-FILLER *THERE* AND WITH CORRECT AGREEMENT

[From text, page 328]

Directions: WRITE FIVE SENTENCES OF YOUR OWN **in which you use *THERE* as a space-filler in the subject territory**. For **each** sentence, use **PLURAL agreement**. Imitate the example.

Example: There **were** many **REASONS** why Gail succeeded.

____

____

____

____

____

Practice C: WRITING SENTENCES USING INDEFINITE PRONOUNS WITH SINGULAR AGREEMENT

[From text, page 328]

Directions: WRITE FIVE SENTENCES OF YOUR OWN **in which you use these five pronouns AS SUBJECT—*EACH, EITHER, NEITHER, EVERYONE,* and *EVERYBODY***. Use only the **present tense** or ***was*** or ***were*** or ***has*** or ***have***.

____

____

____

____

____

Practice D: Writing Sentences with Prepositional Phrases in the Subject Territory

[From text, page 329]

Directions: USE EACH OF THE WORDINGS BELOW AS THE SUBJECT OF A SENTENCE, and use only the **present tense** or ***was*** or ***were*** or ***has*** or ***have***.

The books from the library ______________________________

Land in the mountains ______________________________

A river with minnows ______________________________

The banks of a river ______________________________

A tree with cones ______________________________

The boats on the lake ______________________________

Practice E: Writing Sentences with Plural Subjects Joined by *And*

[From text, page 329]

Directions: WRITE THREE SENTENCES OF YOUR OWN in which there are at least TWO SUBJECTS JOINED BY *AND*. Use only the **present tense** or ***was*** or ***were*** or ***has*** or ***have***.

____

____

____

Practice F: WRITING SENTENCES WITH SUBJECTS JOINED BY *OR*, *EITHER ... OR*, OR *Neither ... Nor*

[From text, page 329]

Directions: USE EACH OF THE WORDINGS BELOW AS THE SUBJECT OF A SENTENCE, and use only the **present tense** or ***was*** or ***were*** or ***has*** or ***have***.

Cereal or muffins ______________________________

Neither these answers nor that one ______________________________

A dog or raccoons ______________________________

Rain or snow flurries ______________________________

The twins or their brother ______________________________

They or I ______________________________